THE CHERRY ORCHARD

Catastrophe and Comedy

TWAYNE'S MASTERWORK STUDIES

Robert Lecker, General Editor

THE CHERRY ORCHARD

Catastrophe and Comedy

Donald Rayfield

TWAYNE PUBLISHERS
An Imprint of Simon & Schuster Macmillan
NEW YORK

Prentice Hall International
LONDON · MEXICO CITY · NEW DELHI · SINGAPORE · SYDNEY · TORONTO

Twayne's Masterwork Series No. 131
Copyright © 1994 by Twayne Publishers, an imprint of Simon & Schuster Macmillan

Twayne Publishers
An Imprint of Simon & Schuster Macmillan
1633 Broadway
New York, NY 10019-6785

Library of Congress Cataloging-in-Publication Data

Rayfield, Donald, 1942–
   The cherry orchard : Catastrophe and comedy / Donald Rayfield.
     p. cm.—(Twayne's masterwork studies ; 131)
   Includes bibliographical references and index.
   ISBN 0-8057-8364-4—ISBN 0-8057-4451-7 (pbk.)
   1. Chekhov, Anton Pavlovich, 1860–1904. Vishnevyi sad. I. Title. II. Series.
PG3455.V53R39 1994
891.72'3—dc20

93-29455
CIP

The paper used in this publication meets the minimum requirements of American National Standard for Information Sciences—Permanence of Paper for Printed Library Materials. ANSI Z39.48-1984.∞ ™

10 9 8 7 6 5 4 3 2 1 (alk. paper)
10 9 8 7 6 5 4 3 2   (pbk.: alk. paper)

Printed in the United States of America.

Wicked dreams abuse the curtained sleep.
Macbeth, *2.1*

Contents

Note on the References and Acknowledgments

I have used Michael Frayn's translation of Anton Chekhov's last play, *The Cherry Orchard*, from his *Chekhov: Plays* (London and New York: Methuen, 1988). I thank Mr. Frayn and and Methuen for permission to quote from this translation of Chekhov's play. I have used my own literal translation when it is needed to clinch the point. All other translations are my own.

In this study I have tried to present everything worth saying of my own and others' thoughts. I wish to thank in particular Alevtina Kuzicheva of the Chekhov Commission of the Russian Academy of Sciences for her generosity with ideas and information, without which my time in Moscow would have been less fruitful. I thank the manuscript section of the Russian State Library, Moscow, for its responsiveness. Ideas have been borrowed, some unwittingly, from colleagues and friends, Russian and non-Russian, notably at two stimulating conferences—in Moscow in 1990 and in Melikhovo in 1992. Other ideas have arisen from seminars with undergraduate students at Queen Mary and Westfield College: I am indebted to the late Vladimir Lakshin and to Miron Petrovsky, Irina Arzhantseva, Alan Gale, Unis Shaikh, Nina Owen, and Corine Brousselle. My wife, Rosalind, produced a shower of inspiring observations, especially on the pertinence of *Macbeth* to Chekhov's play.

I am grateful to Peters, Fraser & Dunlop for providing me with a copy of John Fletcher's *The Apple Orchard*.

Anton Chekhov in 1904.

Chronology: Anton Chekhov's Life and Works

1856   Czar Alexander II proclaims emancipation of Russian serfs.

1860   After Aleksandr (1855–1913) and Nikolai (1859–89), a third son, Anton Pavlovich, is born in the Azov seaport of Taganrog to Pavel Egorovich Chekhov, a shopkeeper of serf origin, and his wife, Evgenia Iakovlevna Chekhova.

1867–1876   Anton Chekhov spends his spare time after school at the shop counter and in the church choir. Taganrog is a thriving cosmopolitan grain port, with a lively Russian theater and music hall, Italian opera, rich Greek merchants, and a picturesque forested hinterland.

1875   Aleksandr and Nikolai Chekhov leave for Moscow University.

1876   The family business goes bankrupt. Pavel and Evgenia Chekhov and their younger children—Maria (1863–1957) and Mikhail (1865–1936)—flee to Moscow. Anton remains in Taganrog on his own to complete his schooling.

1879   Chekhov joins family in Moscow and enrolls in Moscow University's medical school. Sends his first humorous story to the journal *Strekoza* (Dragonfly) and begins to finance his studies and to support his family.

1883   Becomes a regular contributor to Nikolai Leikin's journal *Oskolki* (Fragments), often signing himself as Antosha Chekhonte. Writes but shelves his first play, *Platonov* (now referred to as *Fatherlessness*).

1884   Publishes 20 of 200 pieces written so far in his first book, *Tales of Melpomene*. Graduates as a doctor. Publishes his only novel, *A Shooting Party (or, Drama at the Shoot)*—half-pastiche, half-detective story—in a daily newspaper. The novel is notable (and prophetic) for its fabulous, symbolic neglected garden and trees.

1886   Noticed by established writers, he is commissioned to write serious, substantial stories for the St. Petersburg newspaper *Novoe vremia* (New Times) and has two full-time careers—one medical, one literary. Begins a long friendship with the owner of *Novoe vremia*, Aleksei Suvorin (1834–1912), a right-wing publisher, dramatist, and self-made provincial. Chekhov is tempted to marry Dunia Efros but is too committed to his family. Symptoms of tuberculosis become ominous and unmistakable.

1887   Visits Taganrog and is struck by the deforestation and desolation mining has wreaked on the southern Russian landscape, especially the former "Switzerland of the Don" between Kharkov and the Azov Sea. In the autumn is commissioned to write a play for the Moscow Korsh Theater. *Ivanov*, his first controversial play and his only "tragedy," has limited acclaim and puzzles critics with its moral ambiguity.

1888   The long story "Steppe," his masterpiece, pays tribute to the South and to Russian classical prose. He is awarded the Russian Academy of Science's Pushkin Prize for Literature. Is hereafter paid well enough to write only what and when he wants. His one-act farces, such as *The Bear* and *The Proposal*, have runaway success with professional and amateur actors. Travels to the Crimea and the Caucasus with Suvorin's son.

1889   Publishes a very personal, morbid, first-person account of a doctor facing death, *A Dreary Story*. Hostile critics allege that this work plagiarizes Leo Tolstoy's *Death of Ivan Ilyich* (Tolstoy's influence on Chekhov's writing is now noticeable) and reveals its author's lack of principles. Publishes *The Wood Demon*, a comedy prototype of *Uncle Vania*. Despite his medical ministrations to his brother Nikolai, the latter dies of tuberculosis. His eldest brother, Aleksandr, a talented writer, is an alcoholic.

1890   Undertakes a dangerous journey across Siberia (following the path of the explorer Nikolai Przhevalsky, whose obituary he had written) to the penal colony of Sakhalin, where he single-handedly conducts a sociomedical survey of the population. The trip worsens his tubercular condition, and he partially recuperates on a long sea voyage home, with visits to Japanese and Sri Lankan brothels, Hong Kong, and a burial at sea to distract him. This journey gives his work far greater self-assurance, tolerance, and an existential awareness of life's precariousness and futility: he distances himself from Tolstoy's teachings.

Chronology

<table>
<tr><td>1891</td><td>No sooner back in Russia with two pet mongooses, he travels with the Suvorins to Western Europe. Works on his greatest "Caucasian" story, "The Duel," wherein the traditional Russian arguments between active and acquiescent characters are now neutralized by an idealized portrait of natives and a sympathy for the simple Christian. Is involved in famine relief work.</td></tr>
<tr><td>1892</td><td>Buys an estate at Melikhovo, 45 miles south of Moscow, for himself, his parents, and his sister, Maria. Fights famine and a cholera epidemic among the peasantry, builds schools, and plants trees and still manages to write his most pessimistic and influential story, "Ward No. 6," a portrait of a derelict mental hospital that devours its callous, complacent doctor as well as its idealist patient. Read as an allegory of Russia by Russia's major writers, this story is the first Chekhovian work with political implications.</td></tr>
<tr><td>1893–1895</td><td>The death of Alexander III and accession of Nicholas II raises hopes of creative freedom. Chekhov publishes *The Island of Sakhalin*, a seminal work of social geography, disdained by Moscow academics and ignored by critics. He begins to experiment in his fiction, with each story exploring a new setting, showing the influence of Guy de Maupassant and Emile Zola. Constantly besieged by guests and admirers, leaves Melikhovo on frequent journeys to such destinations as Yalta and Italy. Meets Tolstoy, whom he admires as a man and an artist but not as a thinker. Publishes the melodramatic story "The Black Monk," in which a doomed orchard plays a symbolic part.</td></tr>
<tr><td>1896</td><td>Publishes *The Seagull*, his first mature play and Russia's most modernistic theatrical experience. The play, which is very antagonistic toward conventional theater and the acting profession, fails spectacularly in St. Petersburg. Chekhov vows to forsake theater. The stories "The House with the Mezzanine" and the extensive "My Life" subtly affirm a new technique of subtle narration, in which the first-person protagonist merges with Chekhov's authorial persona, discarding all "isms."</td></tr>
<tr><td>1897</td><td>The unfinished story "Peasants" is desiccated by censors and denounced by Tolstoy as a "sin before the people" for its uncompromising, almost Marxist portrayal of degradation in postfeudal Russia. Chekhov collapses from hemorrhaging of the lungs. Forced by doctors to quit Melikhovo, he travels to Biarritz and Nice in southern France. His political feelings are aroused by France's Dreyfus trial: he respects Zola and breaks for a time with the anti-Semitic Suvorin.</td></tr>
</table>

1898	His father, Pavel Chekhov, dies. Is forced to move to the milder climate of Yalta. Befriends and advises younger prose writers Maksim Gorky and Ivan Bunin. Writes ultra-short, apparently amoral stories such as "About Love." Vladimir Nemirovich-Danchenko persuades Chekhov to allow him to produce *The Seagull* for Konstantin Stanislavsky's new Moscow Arts Theater (MAT). Chekhov meets Olga Knipper, an MAT actress. The story "A Visit to Friends" adumbrates the situation and plot of *The Cherry Orchard*.
1899	*The Wood Demon*, rewritten as *Uncle Vania*, capitalizes on the vogue for Chekhovian drama. His story "Lady with the Lap Dog" becomes the last and most ambiguous word on the nineteenth-century theme of "the adulterous woman." Illness confines Chekhov more and more to Yalta. The social critique of "Peasants" is extended in the stories "In the Gully," "The New Dacha," and "On Official Business."
1900–1902	Illness slows both his gardening and writing. Publishes *Three Sisters*, his most complex play, which conveys his feelings of exile from Moscow and sense of breakup of family in addition to previous dramatic themes of feckless provincial paralysis. Marries Olga Knipper, despite tensions with his sister, Maria. Spends his honeymoon being treated for tuberculosis. Is distressed by Knipper's miscarriage. His new wife acts as a link with Stanislavsky, but disagreements interfere with collaboration. His two last stories—"The Bishop," by consensus the summit of Russian prose and an elegy on death, and "The Bride (or, The Fiancée)," the beginning of quasi-feminist writing and a paean to life—seem to summarize Russia's and the writer's past and query their future. In the summer of 1902 tries to return to central Russia. Resigns from the Academy to protest Gorky's exclusion therefrom.
1903–1904	Russia begins to blunder into ruinous war with Japan and political destabilization. Chekhov, confined to Yalta, composes and revises *The Cherry Orchard*, with a brief visit to Moscow for its celebratory production. He then leaves for the inappropriate German spa of Badenweiler, where medical skills were powerless to prevent his death on 2 July 1904.

LITERARY AND
HISTORICAL CONTEXT

1

Chekhov's Culture and Traditions

Anton Chekhov saw his position in Russian drama and literature as a modest one: the great writers of the previous generation had died—Fyodor Dostoyevski in 1881, Ivan Turgenev in 1884—or, in the case of Leo Tolstoy, had retired from literature to become consciences of the nation. This interregnum in Russia between the classics of the recent past and the conjectural greatness of the future seemed to Chekhov to be like the interregnum in France, where Gustave Flaubert and Stendhal had been succeeded by more populist prose writers such as Emile Zola and Guy de Maupassant. Chekhov saw his task, like theirs, as not to preach or write confessions but to entertain, to stimulate, to respond to public demand with well-crafted stories and plays. Chekhov's genius, of course, led to work of far greater impact and significance than mere entertainment, but his lack of pretension and his refusal to lead, indict, or openly rebel nevertheless mark a break with the past.

Chekhov's origins both as citizen and writer were relatively lowly: he did not belong to the gentry, and his stories mostly avoid the aristocracy, even though his plays are primarily about the landowning classes. His first stories were short, humorous works written for a demanding, newly literate city public. His early readers and editors formed him as a writer—he developed economy with language, precision with details (whether the hunting calendar or the sequence in which flowers appear and birds sing), and authorial reticence. The fame that came to Chekhov from 1887 onward allowed him to write only what and when he wanted, but his early comic work leaves a permanent imprint.

Chekhov's education in the seaport of Taganrog was thorough if conventional. While he was never enthralled by any European writer, his work shows that he was permanently influenced by his *gimnaziia* (grammar school) curriculum. The Greek and Roman philosophers, especially Stoics such as Marcus Aurelius, and the Bible—both the New Testament and the more lyrical and philosophical works of the Old Testament such as Ecclesiastes—influenced even his mature work. While Chekhov was never a believing Christian, his knowledge of Church Slavonic (the language of the the Russian Orthodox liturgy) has led to psalmlike passages in his late work. *The Cherry Orchard* (1904), like much of his work, shows a familiarity with Shakespeare, particularly *Hamlet*, the tragedy and character of procrastination and rebellion most relevant to Russian political and literary life. Like all medical students in Russia at the time, Chekhov had to know German as well as Latin, but the Germanic influence on his work came much later and was limited to the pessimism of Arthur Schopenhauer's philosophy and the new drama of Gerhart Hauptmann. It is clear that Chekhov read French literature for pleasure, and it was writers a decade older than himself—Maupassant and Zola—who had the strongest influence on his work, both technically and in how they viewed literature as a profession. Zola believed the writer a scientist conducting an autopsy, which Chekhov, a medical doctor, found particularly persuasive. Indeed, he had even stronger cause than Zola to see his work as a detached forensic exercise.

Another major influence on Chekhov's evolution as a writer was popular culture. From his schooldays onward, Chekhov was a connoisseur of vaudeville, or the music hall. This was one of the vital strands of Russian cultural life, closely linked with Europe and America, from where operettas such as *The Geisha* or music hall songs such as "Tarara-boom-deay" were absorbed in rapid osmosis. All of this culture was familiar to Chekhov's contemporaries in Russia; much of it is now forgotten. A full understanding of even such mature work as *The Cherry Orchard* is impaired if the operetta, music hall, and folkloric allusions go unmarked.

Chekhov's position in Russian literature is extraordinary not only in the breadth of his culture, from popular to classical, but also in that he never rebelled against his predecessors in the way most Russian writers had. Dostoyevski wrote Nikolai Gogol out of his system in a parricidal frenzy: Chekhov was willingly befriended by the grand old men of his youth—by Nikolay Semyonovich Leskov and Tolstoy. He develops, rather than overthrows, the storytelling and dramatic techniques of Turgenev; he experiments with and modifies Tolstoy's style and ideas but (except in his letters) does not overtly denounce them.

This apprentice's approach to literary tradition, particularly his willingness to incorporate the detached stance of French literature into the very committed role of a Russian writer, made Chekhov's position among his contemporaries difficult, occasionally untenable. His stories and plays are deliberately understated and ambiguous when they seek to be nonjudgmental. Even before the 1917 revolution, Russian critics expected writers not just to analyze the evils of society and miseries of the human condition but to show the potential for good and the "paths to the beautiful." Chekhov's use of irony—where the more heroic his characters, the less convincing are their declarations; where the author reserves his position, or at least leaves the audience and reader to reflect on it—irritated and even infuriated critics. Chekhov's heroic 1890 journey to the penal colony of Sakhalin, which hastened his death, was in part a response to critics who asserted that he did not care about human suffering, that he was a pure artist with no social conscience.

Apart from critical responses, other factors shaped Chekhov's work: censorship, publishers and directors, and the requirements of the market. Russian censorship was politically harsh enough to force Chekhov to change some of Trofimov's speeches that denounce the conditions of the servants and peasants, but in other respects it often gave the writer greater freedom than he enjoyed in Western Europe. It is notable that a play that scandalized Britain—George Bernard Shaw's *Mrs Warren's Profession*—was performed in St. Petersburg with no shock, or that Zola's novel about a young prostitute, *Nana* (1880), was published in Russia before it could appear in France—indeed, it had been banned in the English-speaking world. The Russian Orthodox Church failed to exert the same moral and dogmatic pressure that the Catholic Church had in France, Spain, and Italy or the Protestant churches had in Scandinavia, Great Britain, and the United States. The plays of Alexandre Dumas fils in France or the work of Charles Dickens and William Makepeace Thackeray in England were subject to an unwritten but effective ecclesiastical censorship that operated through commercial publishers and lending libraries. The Russian state, however authoritarian, was largely secular.

Russian censorship was furthermore *pre*-censorship: a writer and publisher knew in advance what was permissible and what was not. There was little risk of confiscation, ruin, or prosecution after publication or performance—factors that greatly inhibited literature and the theater in Western Europe and America. Censorship was also largely in the hands of writers themselves and was predictable enough for writers to cope with. Chekhov benefited from the growth of a newly literate public and the rise of major publishers such as Aleksei Suvorin, who supplied the station bookstalls on the new railways. The "thick" monthly journals increased in number, size, political diversity, and readership throughout the 1880s, despite the reactionary domestic politics of Alexander III.

The Russian theater was another matter. For the early part of Chekhov's writing career (up to 1887) the medium was dominated by the state-subsidised theaters that were conservative in their repertoire, preferring European classics or contemporary popular plays to new serious drama, and very subservient to the prejudices of leading actors and actresses. Only when private theaters were developed by wealthy amateurs from the merchant classes, such as Konstantin Stanislavsky, and the cult of the director overcame the resistance of the acting profession, could new drama, such as Chekhov's *Seagull*, be performed without being sabotaged and destroyed by the conservative acting establishment that it provoked and attacked. In Chekhov's last years, repertory theater in the provinces followed the lead of Stanislavsky's Moscow Arts Theater and new drama like *The Cherry Orchard*, hitherto considered outlandishly experimental, could command wide, unsubsidized audiences.

Perhaps the most extraordinary feature of the Russian theater in the nineteenth century, however, is that virtually no writer, with the exception of the playwright Nikolai Ostrovsky (who wrote 47 plays largely on the dramatic home life of the merchant classes), was a fulltime professional dramatist. The theater was a stage in a writer's development: in the case of Aleksandr Pushkin and Turgenev, drama was a transitional genre by which the poet graduated to narrative prose; in the case of Gogol or Tolstoy, tragedy and comedy became vehicles at a moment when the storyteller felt he had to preach to a live audience; in the work of the symbolist poets, such as Fyodor Sologub, Innokenty Annensky, or Aleksandr Blok, lyrical verse gave way to drama when the divided self of the poet's persona appeared to require dramatic confrontation. With the outstanding exception of Gogol's comedies, the disadvantage of this dilettantism was that Russian plays were often difficult to stage, taking little notice of the practicalities of the set, audience demand, or actors' preferences; the advantages were those of fools who rush in where angels fear to tread. Still, even before Chekhov Russian drama was notable for its extraordinary originality: from Pushkin's "little tragedies" and Gogol's almost entirely male comic menace to Annensky's pseudo-Euripidean tragedies of poetic inspiration, these amateur playwrights appeared to anticipate—because they demanded it—the stage of theaters to come.

In this sense Chekhov is typical of Russian theater. His interest in theater was profound, and many of his closest friends were actors and actresses; yet he never acted, and while his farces are brilliant intensifications of French and Russian farce technique, his major plays show every sign of being the work of a prose writer who refuses to sacrifice the privileges of narrative prose and denies conventional actors the chance to show their talent. Chekhov's motivation was in fact antagonistic. His early journalism shows how much he loathed the classical declamation and histrionics of "great acting" such as Sarah Bernhardt. His plays were partly written—*The Seagull* (1896) only too obviously so—to puzzle and antagonize actors and audiences. The challenge of a hostile text worked only when matched by the director's rebellious new theater: Stanislavsky and Chekhov were united in their determination to subjugate the actor to the text and the words to the overall mood of the staging. More than any of his Russian predecessors, Chekhov succeeded, by finding a theater that at least partially agreed with him, in making the antitheatrical play force a theatrical revolution. *The Cherry Orchard* is the ultimate theatrical coup d'état.

An open mind about genre, about the distinction between comedy and tragedy, is the best attribute of Russian theater in the nineteenth century. We find this openness and ambiguity in Chekhov's ideology. Despite censorship, most Russian writers centered their work on Russia's political predicaments: whether to become a Western culture or a Slavic one, whether to aim for reform, even revolution, or to consolidate the Byzantine and feudal heritage. Even esthetes such as Turgenev found it difficult to exclude such questions from a classic assessment of the meaning of life. While Chekhov is not utterly silent on these historic questions, he responds with reticence. Even a contentious story such as "Ward No. 6," in which a complacent doctor is imprisoned and killed in a hellish provincial mental hospital, was interpreted only by readers, not by the author, as a political allegory. Chekhov's dramatic heroes willingly philosophize on hopes for the future and mistakes of the past, and the audience senses that the work's real focus is not on what these characters say but on why they say what they do. Chekhov's letters only hint that he preferred freedom to restriction, the comforts of technology to the discomforts of asceticism; that he was liberal rather than conservative or revolutionary (and note that *liberal* in Russian could be almost a term of abuse).

The key to Chekhov's underlying thought is to be found not in his literary loyalties but in two other occupations. First he was a doctor, and the first lessons in philosophy he learnt were medical: not to become too involved in the suffering of the patient; to diagnose objectively, prognosticate cautiously, and treat conservatively. Medicine provides themes for many of his stories. The progress of a disease makes plot and character, teaches acceptance of death, suspects morbidity in genius, and humbles the author-artist. An attentive reading of

Chekhov's Culture and Traditions

The Cherry Orchard, Chekhov's only play without a doctor, betrays the dramatist as forensic scientist. For Chekhov, medicine was a legitimate wife and literature an illicit mistress: the demands of science overrode the claims of art. Until he became too ill to do more than write, Chekhov spent as much time treating the sick—his relatives or the peasantry—as he did reading and writing.

Chekhov's other preoccupation, after buying the estate at Melikhovo in 1892, was gardening on a large scale—his journeys to France were typically to plant nurseries, not to attend writers' reunions. The garden or orchard (both *sad* in Russian) is the setting for many encounters in stories and plays, and its making and unmaking is often the central theme. Chekhov subscribed to gardening journals, and we can argue that even the nonlinear, circular structure of many of his plays and stories owes more to the principles of garden design—where boundaries must be concealed and ends merged with beginnings—than to the linear conventions of literary plotting. Chekhov planted forests, including a cherry orchard of his own. When he was forced to move to Yalta and sell Melikhovo, the joy of planting his Yalta garden was overshadowed by the tragedy of the lost estate, where the new purchaser felled a large part of the timber (the Yalta garden still survives as an exotic monument to a man whose feeling for trees equalled his feeling for theater). Trees are the heroes and victims of his stories and plays, so much so that Chekhov has to be singled out as Europe's first ecological writer in many senses of the word: his main interest is in the ecology of human beings—how a random assortment of personalities results in a way of living together—and the ecology of nature and man, in which one is destroyed by the other to their mutual impoverishment. *The Cherry Orchard*, like so many other Chekhov works, numbers the trees as part of its cast of characters.

In the widest ecological sense, we should note that Chekhov's personal life, and therefore his language and the raw psychological material for his work, was unusually restricted. Although he traveled to Europe and Asia, foreign settings play a peripheral role in his work. He rarely uses even the capital city setting of St. Petersburg. Each play and story has precisely delineated familiar coordinates, often identifiable to the point of a grid reference in space and a chronological point in time—and usually stemming from a personal experience of place. Thus Moscow and the belt of countryside along the railway line to the South—to Yalta and to Taganrog—is the spinal column of Chekhov's work: the outskirts of Kharkov in *The Cherry Orchard* and the countryside in *Uncle Vania* (1899) are literally close to home.

Most of Chekhov's life was spent in the company of his parents, brother Mikhail, and sister. He married only when he was dying; he was more often host to importunate visitors than guest. His 4,000 extant letters corroborate the details of his literary work, and the letters of his close friends and his elder brothers have shown how the very texture of Chekhov's dramatic dialogue is bound up with the language of his close family circle. Family language makes for family themes. Because Chekhov is not a confessional writer—he does not transpose autobiography directly into art—it would be futile to use his life history and his art to verify each other; nevertheless, his correspondence and the memoirs of contemporaries form a context for a deeper reading of his stories and plays.

2

The Importance of *The Cherry Orchard*

The Cherry Orchard is important for three reasons: first, for its intrinsic textual richness, its linguistic power and subtlety as a piece of dramatic prose; second, because of its crucial position in Russian cultural history as the culmination of all "realist" nineteenth-century fiction and as the first classic of a new, arguably "symbolist" or "absurdist" literature; third, because of its seminal role in the evolution of twentieth-century theater.

An appreciation of the play's dramatic power is of course best gained from watching different stagings of the text by good actors and great directors, at best in the original Russian, at least in professional and competent translations. The play fomented controversy among producers, actors, critics, and audiences for decades after its first performance because it is saturated with many different, apparently incompatible, elements. On a primary level the play fulfills all the conventional requirements of classical and of realist drama. It aligns the action with time, from hopeful spring to despairing autumn. It has a crux to the plot that remains unresolved until the end of the third act—Will the estate be sold or saved? It has couples who seem destined to be married, servants who fail to serve, a heroine with both grave flaws and charisma, who runs the gamut from tomfoolery to tragic rhetoric. Its plot is built around a tried and tested dramatic device: the disturbance caused by the return of long-lost relatives to a hitherto peaceful family nest. It uses the "skeleton in the closet" technique of an unmentionable tragedy that occurred years before the play begins. It has pathos, wit, articulated emotion.

In its superficially conventional structure, *The Cherry Orchard* thus appears to perfect four centuries of European comedy and incorporate many of the traditional formulas of classical tragedy—fatal flaw, hubris, catastrophe, and nemesis, though not the fourth purifying stage of catharsis. On a specifically Russian level, it seems to tackle issues that are both contemporary (to the 1890s and 1900s) and recurrent: the disinheritance of the landowning nobility by their own fecklessness, the disillusionment with the emancipatory reforms of four decades earlier, the debate on the redemption of Russia, the arguments on whether radical thought or Western capitalism holds the key to the future, and the contrast of hide-bound Russian and freethinking French moral values. All these themes had been at the core of Russian literature, especially drama, for more than a century, since Catherine the Great encouraged dramatists to reflect and question the inhabitants and mores of her empire.

Into this conventional warp, however, *The Cherry Orchard* brings an unconventional woof: the constant transition from comedy to pathos, the oscillation of language from music hall vulgarity to prose poetry, the assignment of a subtle idiolect—a personal way of speaking—to each character, the divorce of consequence from action, of cause from effect. The total failure of characters to listen forces evolution on drama. Even more extraordinary is the wealth of stage direction, the richness required in props and decorations, sound effects, and even smell, to the point that we are beginning in Chekhov's drama to deal with Wagnerian concepts of art—a synthesis of music and of visual art with text. Chekhov has refused to abandon the baggage of a story writer when he composes drama. At the same time he has abandoned the privileged, judgmental role of the *raisonneur*, the author as commentator, and the audience is left to grasp the work's philosophical and moral import on its own. This is all the more true of this play, wherein Chekhov has for the first time omitted the character of the doctor, to whom the audience looks for interpretation and objectivity. Most of Chekhov's audiences had seen his other plays and read his narrative prose. *The Cherry Orchard* resumes the themes of all his drama and dramatizes much of his prose: its richness is thus intertextual and stems from a store of reading that is common to audience and author. By intertextual allusion, by just a few triggering phrases, Chekhov incorporates and plays with themes, characters, and ideas from his own work; from that of contemporaries, whether Maupassant or Friedrich Nietzsche; and from the classics. Drama had never before been so rich in allusion to other texts.

The Cherry Orchard addressed important contemporary issues via its protagonists' arguments—arguments about action or inaction, evolution or revolution, that persist to this day. The starry-eyed radicalism of Trofimov, the self-serving capitalism of Lopakhin, and the intuitive deafness to reason on the part of the orchard's owners (who nevertheless are wise in their foolishness) are just as relevant to today's Russia as to yesterday's; such stances and conflicts set out permanently irresoluble dilemmas for the human condition. The play can be read as a conflict between duty and desire, between degeneracy and regeneration, between hope and despair, between conflicting illusions, or between nature and mankind. Above all, however, it can be read as an evocation of honest pessimism about the outcome of all these conflicts, with only a glimmer of hope and no false consolations. Chekhov had all his life tried to educate his Russian public not to regard the writer and dramatist as a Moses or John the Baptist, and in *The Cherry Orchard* he makes a supreme effort to disabuse them of this illusion.

What Chekhov did not foresee as he struggled to complete the play while beset by a worsening illness was that *The Cherry Orchard* would, even more than *Three Sisters* (1901), be recognized as the start of a new type of drama. In this play comedy has become cruel enough to deal with tragic situations; dramatic silences (like musical rests) have acquired the same importance as utterances; and there is a suggestion of a numinous presence—of Time or of Nature—with a heroic status denied to the human protagonists. Drama has become so rich in mood and implied messages that an all-powerful director is needed to subordinate the actors in a single interpretation, just as classical music in the nineteenth century became too complex for the orchestral players to interpret a composition without the inexorable baton of the conductor. By blurring the boundaries between the genres—between comedy and tragedy, between prose narrative and drama—and by introducing musical values—a structure of recurrent motifs, of an end that reiterates the beginning—Chekhov's *Cherry Orchard* became a progenitor of radical theater first in Russia and then all over the world.[1] Chekhov hastened the development of a director-led theater company in which interpretation of the text, not the cult of the actor, came to dominate the performance—a theater whose methods have led straight to cinematic and televisual dramatic techniques, where individual subtleties in characterization, visual background, and music all interact in a way undreamed of before Chekhov.

The apparent contradiction of a play that is simultaneously comic and tragic is a fact of the modernist drama of Samuel Beckett, Eugène Ionesco, Antonin Artaud, and Anton Chekhov. Only in this century has the theater been able to flesh out the ideas of Søren Kierkegaard, whose *(Concluding) Unscientific Postscript* states, "Pathos that is not reinforced by the comic is illusion; the comic that is not reinforced by pathos is immaturity. Seen pathetically, a second has infinite value; seen comically, ten thousand years are a mere flash of foolery like yesterday; and yet time, in which the existing individual finds himself, is made up of such parts."[2] Thus Chekhov's use of time—from the melancholy moments of the breaking string, to the absurd speculation about 200 years in the future—incarnates Kierkegaard in *The Cherry Orchard*, because the play's action suddenly expands to encompass the historical past (the 1861 emancipation) and the speculative future (the utopia to come). The characters' preoccupations seem petty against such a time scale, yet they are suddenly transfixed, as if at a critical stage in a long process.

3

Critical Reception

The Cherry Orchard began to reverberate in Russian literature even before it was performed or published. The first reaction, in November 1903, was that of the state censor Vasili Vereshchagin, who found two passages of social criticism in Trofimov's speeches in act 2 too outspoken and forced Chekhov to substitute less biting passages. In December, when Chekhov came to Moscow to attend rehearsals, the great director of the Moscow Arts Theater Konstantin Stanislavsky, and many of his actors appeared to react to the play as though it were a tragedy or a straightforward political diatribe. Stanislavsky's telegram of congratulations ended, "We wept in the last act."[1] His wife, Maria Lilina, who was to play Ania, dared to contradict the author's subtitle "comedy": "It's a tragedy, whatever outlet to a better life you reveal in the last act. . . . I wept, as a woman."[2] A little later she intuited, "*The Cherry Orchard* is not a play, but a work of music, a symphony." Vladimir Nemirovich-Danchenko, Stanislavsky's second in command, had for 12 years enjoyed Chekhov's trust. He had achieved a reputation in Russia as a playwright and sacrificed this career to serve the Moscow Arts Theater: his plays, such as *Tsena zhizni* (The Price of Life) of 1889, developed the merchant dramas of Nikolai Ostrovsky with a French vaudeville lightness and, despite their lack of original spark or subtlety, were apparently genuinely admired by Chekhov. Nemirovich-Danchenko sensed (in an extravagant telegram to Chekhov) that they had "overdone the tears."[3] Chekhov stressed the play's vaudeville qualities: the tears of the Ranevskaia household were only metaphorical. At the same time he edited the text to bring out the sensitivity of his capitalist Lopakhin. Chekhov was prepared to incorporate an actor's improvisation only if it enhanced the ludicrous side of the play. Some actors realized how complex the play was: A. L. Vishnevsky called it "the most expensive lace . . . the most difficult of your plays to perform."[4]

The play was first performed on 17 January 1904 to celebrate the twenty-fifth anniversary of Chekhov's literary career, but the sight of the dying author, unable to stand, wanly acknowledging applause, was hardly festive. The interpretation of the play as a tragic swan song was linked with the spectacle of the playwright's lugubrious last bow. Nemirovich-Danchenko had packed the theater with a claque of spectators (known as "angels") standing behind the legitimate seated audience; many of them were Chekhov's Crimean neighbors—emaciated tubercular young men from Yalta—and their sobs as the play ended to the sound of the last blows of the ax on the cherry trees cast an elegiac pall over the performance.[5] Chekhov's reported reaction was annoyance: "It's all wrong, the play and the performance. That's not what I saw, and they couldn't understand what I wanted."[6] Yet over the 1904 season the theater could not believe its production had betrayed the author: "Never in my theatrical career do I remember seeing an audience react like that to the slightest detail of drama, genre, psychology, as today," Nemirovich-Danchenko telegraphed to Chekhov. "The overall tone of the performance has splendid assurance, precision, talent. More than any other of your plays, the success is due to the author, regardless of the theater."[7]

Only after Chekhov's death did Nemirovich-Danchenko concede that they had misinterpreted the play: "We didn't fully understand his subtle writing. Chekhov was refining realism to the point of symbols, and the theater took a long time to find this delicate weft in Chekhov's work."[8] One perceptive reviewer, the dramatist Aleksandr

Amfiteatrov, insisted, "For all its great success neither the public nor the critics had grasped all its charm; they will take a very long time discovering one depth after another, sinking deeper and deeper into it, loving it and becoming used to it."[9] Amfiteatrov's review was one of the most penetrating: he realized that Chekhov was not to be understood as a political partisan or a social arbiter, that Ranevskaia and Gaev were not the traditional bad landowners rightfully deprived of their property: "The Gaevs perish not in revolt against modern times, but because fate has come to pass: a race is dying out."

Throughout the season, until Chekhov's death in July, there were some 80 reviews of the Moscow Arts Theater's performances. On the whole, the wittiest were the most negative. The doyenne of symbolist salons and head of the anti-Chekhovian school of criticism, Zinaida Gippius (writing as "Anton the Extreme"), dismissed the play as unperformable.[10] A year before she had caricatured the Chekhovian play this way: "It's raining. Leaves are falling. People are drinking tea with jam. They set out a game of patience. They're very bored. They drink, and a drunk laughs quietly for a long time. They're bored again. Sometimes a man feels a sexual urge, makes a pass, and says, 'Voluptuous woman!' They then drink tea again, are bored, and finally die, sometimes of an illness, sometimes by shooting themselves."[11]

The majority of critics, however, agreed with the Moscow Arts Theater: this, said Vlas Doroshevich, "was a comedy in name, a drama in content."[12] It was, he said, a narrative poem: the landowner Ranevskaia and her family were *morituri* (doomed to die). Russia's symbolists, constantly feuding with realism, were, however, detecting in Chekhov not a boring student of reality but a fellow poet mourning the destruction of beauty and the hatefulness of life. The signal was given in the spring of 1904 by the poet, novelist, manifesto writer, and theoretician Andrei Bely. While other symbolists (e.g., the self-proclaimed maestro Valeri Briusov) felt that the play was artifice and that only act 3 had real dramatic impact, Bely in an influential article proclaimed that Chekhov had married realism and symbolism, making the play "a continuous link between the fathers and the children. . . . In act 3 . . . Chekhov's devices crystallize; a family drama takes place in the hall, while in the back room, lit by candles, masks of horror dance in frenzy. . . . [W]hat from a distance seem to be shadowy cracks turn out to be openings into eternity."[13] In 1907 Bely redefined the play: "realism made transparent, naturally fused with symbolism."

In a letter to Chekhov, Vsevolod Meierkhold—the "dark genius" of the Russian theater and once a protégé of Stanislavsky but now a Lucifer cast out into St. Petersburg by the Moscow Arts Theater—claimed *The Cherry Orchard* as authentic symbolist repertory: "I don't much like the Moscow performance of this play. . . . Your play is as abstract as a Tchaikovsky symphony. And a director should use his ear above all to grasp it. In act 3 to the sound of idiotic stamping—and that stamping should be audible—Horror enters, unnoticed by the people. The cherry orchard is sold. They dance. 'It's sold!' They dance. And so on to the end. . . . When one reads plays by foreign authors, you stand apart by your originality. In drama, too, the West will have to learn from you."[14] Meierkhold worshiped Chekhov; he had played Treplev in *The Seagull* and, before his break with Nemirovich-Danchenko and Stanislavsky, was apparently the actor for whom the part of Tuzenbakh in *Three Sisters* was written. It seems that Meierkhold was encouraged by Chekhov's response to his alternative views and felt them to be part of a dialogue. Meierkhold is reported to have told A. K. Gladkov, "Do you know who first sowed doubts in me that not all the paths of the Moscow Arts Theater were right? Anton Chekhov. He disagreed with a lot in the theater, much he criticized outright."

Meierkhold's views on the symbolist nature of *The Cherry Orchard* were spectacularly graphic but never realized in the theater. His own three performances of the play in the Black Sea port of Kherson in February 1904 apparently differed little from the Moscow Arts Theater style he had been trained in. Moving to St. Petersburg and joining forces with the great actress-director Vera Komissarzhevskaia, Meierkhold found himself forced to submit to her view that *The Cherry Orchard* was unplayable except in the Moscow Arts Theater tradition. Nevertheless, in 1906 Meierkhold did sketch an alternative mise-en-scène for the play, which was never produced, despite the 30 years of his career still left to run. The ideas he set out in a 1908 article of are persuasive: Epikhodov, Iasha, and Duniasha he saw as the circus figures of Pierrot, Harlequin, and Colombine, who figure prominently in French and Russian symbolist poetry, in Pablo Picasso's blue period, and in Igor Stravinsky's *Petrushka*.[15] Meierkhold's vision of Ranevskaia identifies her as the life force.

The progressive, realist camp who saw in Maksim Gorky's *Lower Depths* the real future of drama and revolution tended to dismiss the play as did Gorky: "Nothing new. Everything—moods, ideas, if you can call them that, characters—are to be found in the earlier plays. Of course it's beautiful, and raw anguish on the stage hits the audience. But what the anguish is about, I don't know."[16] Others as subjective as the symbolists reinterpreted Chekhov's play to suit their views: typical in its breathtaking naïveté is a letter Chekhov received from Viktor Baranovsky, a radical student in the provinces: "I heard . . . a call to an active, energetic life of ferment, to bold, fearless struggle—and so to the end of the play I felt intense pleasure. Lopakhin and the student are friends going arm in arm towards that bright star."[17] Many reviewers assumed that if the Ranevskaia household lost its estate deservedly, then Lopakhin or Trofimov were rightful heirs and would create "a future on the wreck of the old."[18] The ambiguity and irony of Chekhov's stance escaped the radicals, as it had for the previous 18 years, ever since Chekhov's neurotic idealist and villain Ivanov (in the play of the same name) first taxed their judgment with his equivocations.

Powerful disparagement was also heard: the most consistent for 50 years to come was from Chekhov's disciple, the great writer Ivan Bunin. He acknowledged Chekhov's supremacy in the short story but, like Tolstoy, felt that the plays were embarrassingly ignorant and incompetent. In vain, Chekhov's defenders pointed out that you did not have to be a nobleman to write about the landed gentry, that strict social realism was not Chekhov's aim. Bunin was upset by Soviet ideology hijacking the Moscow Arts Theater and the "progressive" speeches of Chekhov's characters. Bunin's loathing of *The Cherry Orchard* is important because it formed an undercurrent of opinion that still flows in Russia today. Bunin wrote, "There were never any orchards in Russia that were entirely given over to cherry trees and there's nothing wonderful about cherry trees. . . . Ranevskaia is supposed to be a landowner and yet a Parisian, she either weeps hysterically or laughs. . . . It's also quite implausible that Lopakhin should have these profitable trees cut down with such stupid haste before the former owner has even left the house. . . . Firs is fairly plausible, but the rest is unbearable."[19]

The breakup of the symbolist movement on the eve of World War I and the Bolsheviks' use of the theater as ideological centers turned *The Cherry Orchard* first into an unquestionable classic and then into a vehicle for illustrating the inevitability of the old order's collapse. Russian criticism concentrated on textual and intertextual problems, demonstrating the kinship of Chekhov's drama to the "new drama" that arose on the fringes of Western Europe—in Norway, Sweden, and Russia—so that the trio of Henrik Ibsen, August Strindberg, and Anton Chekhov took on a misleading similarity, as dramatists who protested against not only the congealed conventions of the theater but also the hypocrisy and oppression of bourgeois societies. Survivors of the formalist school made only modest inroads into such a simplistic view: the Bulgarian scholar Petr Bitsilli pointed out how daringly Chekhov uses conventional devices such as eavesdropping and soliloquy in *The Cherry Orchard*; Sergei Balukhaty emphasized the lyrical structure and demotion of the exterior world. But Soviet criticism had to subordinate all insights to one task—to prove that great prerevolutionary dramatists were humanists heralding a new dawn, entry to a Promised Land.

For this reason the current of rejection never waned. St. Petersburg poets sensed Chekhov's indifference to their city. The poet Anna Akhmatova was notorious for her dismissal of Chekhov's "grayness": one might suspect that the dislike was self-defense, for many of Akhmatova's early poems are condensed versions of ironic Chekhovian narratives. But the poet Osip Mandelstam, in an unbroadcast radio talk he prepared in 1935 while in exile in Voronezh, articulated his dislike: "A biologist would call the Chekhovian principle ecological. Cohabitation is the decisive factor in Chekhov. In his dramas there is no action—just contiguity and the consequent unpleasantnesses. Recently I went to the Voronezh Town Theater in time for act 3 of *The Cherry Orchard*. The actors were putting on their makeup and resting in the dressing rooms. . . . On the whole, the ruins of the play, backstage, were not bad. After acting Chekhov the actors came offstage as if chilled and a little shifty. The correlation of theater and so-called life in Chekhov is that of a chill to good health."[20]

To those who suffered starvation, persecution, and execution, the predicaments of Chekhov's characters seemed trivial: even after the collapse of the Soviet Union, the satirist Viacheslav Pietsukh has a character exclaim, "Ditherers, bastards, they had a bad life, did they? I'll bet they wore excellent overcoats, knocked back the Worontsoff vodka with caviar, mixed with lovely women, those reptiles philosophized from morning to night for want of anything to do—and then they say they have a bad life, you see? You sons of bitches ought to be in the clutches of a planned economy, you should be brought to an Executive Committee's attention—they'd show you what a cherry orchard was!"[21]

Abroad, Chekhov's reputation depended on two elements: the theatrical climate and the quality, even availability, of translations. In Slavonic cultures the theatrical climate was favorable, and there were literati familiar with Russian. Not surprisingly, the first performances of *The Cherry Orchard* abroad were in Bulgaria (1904) and Bohemia and Moravia (1905). But the nationalistic theater could catch only the "Russianness" and little else; the self-confidence of translators such as the Czech Boleslav Prusík resulted in ludicrously poor translation. In 1911 England was the first major Western European country to stage *The Cherry Orchard*, at first in an imperfect translation by Constance Garnett. The actors solemnly misinterpreted the morality: the English Duniasha was shocked at Charlotta's supposed illegitimacy. Critics found the play "stationary," "queer, outlandish, and even silly." They cited its "fantastic trivialities" and, at their most charitable, assumed it was a display of Russian temperament that no English actor was ready for.[22] (They unwittingly agreed with Chekhov, who had always assumed his drama was of purely local interest.) Half the audience had left the theater by act 3. The few receptive spectators were Russian specialists like Maurice Baring or innovative dramatists like George Bernard Shaw. Baring followed the progressive Russian interpretation, compared the play with Molière's *Le Misanthrope* (*The Misanthropist*) in its lack of violent action, and insisted that the play had to be seen, not read, for the sake of the "hundred effects that make themselves felt on the boards."[23] Shaw was extravagant: "When I hear a play of Chekhov's I want to tear my own up." He called *The Cherry Orchard* the "most important production in England since that of *A Doll's House.*"[24] His *Heartbreak House* (1919) was to pay explicit tribute to Chekhov's comedy.

World War I and the Revolution presented Russia in a militant, heroic light and led critics to discard Chekhov as irrelevant to modern times and his Russia as an ephemeral and uninteresting setting. When *The Cherry Orchard* was again staged in England, in a slightly better version by George Calderon in 1920, it was still judged to be "a decadent ritual," at best "a philosophical essay." Only major innovators responded with enthusiasm. Virginia Woolf declared after watching *The Cherry Orchard* that she felt "like a piano played upon at last . . . all over the keyboard and with the lid left open."[25] The novelist Frank Swinnerton considered *The Cherry Orchard* to be the best of Chekhov's plays for its "most beautifully varied . . . snatches of idle, puzzled, irrelevant talk."[26] Irish writers, like Shaw, saw common ground between Ranevskaia's household and decaying Irish estates. Very few, notably the dramatist and director Granville Barker, who had seen Chekhov produced in Moscow, understood that Stanislavskian acting principles were inseparable from Chekhov's textual innovations: they welcomed the play as a means of carrying out a similar revolution in the English theater.

In the United States Chekhov's plays were read a decade before they were produced, and most critical opinion derided them. The critic Storm Jameson in 1914 concluded that Chekhov was no great dramatist but "by virtue of the complexity of life . . . and an unresting note of revolt . . . a great artist."[27] When a 1915 anthology of "modern masterpieces" included *The Cherry Orchard*, an anonymous reviewer complained, "Why this streak of abstract life is included in a collection . . . is hard to say. . . . [I]t is a lazy dream of idle aristocrats . . . mere portrayal of inept circumstances. . . . [T]o plod through Chekhov's cerebral abullitions . . . the rankest American amateur would be suspected of softening of the cerebellum."[28] In 1923 New

Yorkers saw *The Cherry Orchard*, produced in Russian by the Moscow Arts Theater, with Chekhov's widow, Olga Knipper, playing Ranevskaia and also assisting English-language productions of other Chekhov plays, notably *Three Sisters*. A few critics saw in the aging Knipper-Chekhova merely Junoesque posing, but makers of opinion, such as Edmund Wilson, became apostles of Chekhovian drama, declaring the comedy one of "ineptitude touched with the tragedy of all human failure."[29]

Only after the ponderous performances of the Moscow Arts Theater abroad (by both Stanislavsky's "Soviet" and Vasili Kachalov's "émigré" troupes) had given way to more confident English and American productions did critics and directors begin to see the comedy implicit in *The Cherry Orchard*. Brooks Atkinson in the *New York Times* in 1928 concluded that "despite the melancholy of the conclusion, this comedy . . . sealed an epoch . . . stream of consciousness. . . . [N]othing since *The Cherry Orchard* has woven the new method into such a luminous pattern of beguiling life."[30] By 1933 Tyrone Guthrie in his London production (yet another translation by Charles Butler) had declared Chekhov to be "a thoroughly amusing and flippant dramatist"[31] and based his comedienne's Ranevskaia on Knipper's performance. The influential Miss Le Gallienne productions in the 1940s compromised by making *The Cherry Orchard* a "tragicomedy in which the hero and villain were both aspects of progress and the victim was beauty."[32] In England, too, James Agate had swung opinion in 1925 by declaring it "one of the great plays of the world" and "a comedy of guesswork,"[33] thereby rescuing Chekhov from the contempt of populist critics (e.g., the *Daily Express*: "This silly, tiresome, boring comedy. . . . I know of no reason why this fatuous drivel should be translated at all. There is no plot. The cherry orchard is for sale, and certain dull people are upset because it must be sold").[34]

Germany was one of the first countries to appreciate Chekhov's drama. His play *Ivanov* has such striking echoes in Gerhart Hauptmann's *Einsame Menschen* (*Lonely People*) that it is tempting to see Chekhov imitated in it. Rainer Maria Rilke, spellbound after seeing *The Seagull* at the Moscow Arts Theater, wrote plays such as *Das tägliche Leben* (Daily Life), in which a Mascha, dressed in black, was enthralled by the artist hero. In February 1906 the Moscow Arts Theater (including Knipper) performed in Russian in Berlin: they brought with them the only two Chekhov plays—*Uncle Vania* and *Three Sisters*—then available in German. But their performance was shattering: the notoriously tight-lipped Hauptmann burst into tears in the hall and shrieked in the foyer that this was the greatest stage experience of his life; others, such as the poet Christian Morgenstern, were moved to tears. This created a climate that would be favorable to Chekhov's *The Cherry Orchard* as yet another example of *Stimmungstheater* (mood theater). Despite wartime Russophobia, *The Cherry Orchard* was first performed in German in Vienna in 1916 and again in Munich in 1917. The novelist and dramatist Lion Feuchtwanger had a hand in polishing the German version. He cryptically declared the play "a gloomy mirror of the human spirit which is measuring its limits against the limitless."[35] When the Moscow Arts Theater returned to Germany in 1922, however, it again omitted *The Cherry Orchard* (as it had *The Seagull*), but scorn for Russian inertia was so ingrained that Chekhov's mature plays were rarely performed until well after World War II, and Nazi hostility to all things Slav had prevented significant appreciation of *The Cherry Orchard* in Germany, even though Chekhov was not banned under Hitler. A divided Germany brought a divided view of *The Cherry Orchard*: the Tübingen production of 1947 was slapstick; the East Berlin version of 1950 was coarse, alienating, and Brechtian.

France had esteemed the Russian novel earlier than any other foreign culture, yet, despite the efforts of the translator Denis Roche, reaction to Chekhov had been muted. He was seen primarily as a disciple of Maupassant. The French lack of interest justifies Chekhov's protest to his wife against allowing a translation of *The Cherry Orchard*: "Why translate my play into French? It's crazy, the French won't understand anything about Ermolai [Lopakhin] or the sale of the estate and will only be bored." "I can't forbid it, let anyone who wants translate, it will still be pointless."[36] Not until 1921 was a major play of Chekhov's professionally staged in Paris, and despite the success of *The Seagull, Uncle Vania*, and *Three Sisters* in 1929, *The Cherry Orchard* had to wait until 1944 before it was staged at all. This neglect is all the more surprising when we consider that the French director Georges Pitoëff was of Russian origin and had studied under Stanislavsky and Meierkhold. He had been present at the first performance of *The Cherry Orchard* on 17 January 1904, and between 1915 and 1920, while in exile in Switzerland, he had translated the play into French. (The Roche version was rehearsed in Paris in 1914 but aborted when war broke out.) The absurdist dramatist Arthur Adamov translated several of Chekhov's plays, and his essays collected in the 1964 volume *Ici et maintenant* (Here and Now) show that he regarded *The Cherry Orchard* as the first progenitor of comedy where language fails its primary functions. "Chekhov's characters," he said, "don't say what they think at any given moment but what forms a sort of continual scheme of their thinking."[37] It is the falsity of Chekhov's characters' speeches that made for Adamov potential tragedy comic.

In 1954 Jean-Louis Barrault won acclaim for *The Cherry Orchard*, which he put forward as the greatest of Chekhov's plays: "The play's action actually unfolds through silence and, aside from the poem-tirades which are separate, the dialogues exist, as in music, only to make the silence resound."[38] The delay in presenting the play to the French was evidently justified, for Barrault had catapulted his spectators straight into a modern view of the play as a play around the unspoken, as a musical structure not primarily about the fate of human individuals. Barrault's explanatory remarks are the most illuminating of any made by an actor-director, even more profound than Stanislavsky's. "It is a play about time," Barrault wrote. "And therefore it doesn't matter whether the storyline is Russian or Japanese." Although Barrault paid tribute to the Russian spirit "on the boundaries of East and West" for revealing a way of "penetrating and perceiving the imperceptible passage of time," he insisted on its universality as a play about time: "The action never slackens; it is tense, solid, for, I repeat, every minute is full. Every minute has its own saturation, but not with dialogues, but silence, life itself passing."

By breaking down the framework of a social message, Chekhov's ideological impact, Barrault asserted, was like acupuncture: the impact was out of all proportion to the force exerted. The three male protagonists—Gaev, Lopakhin, and Trofimov—Barrault saw in terms of time as past, present, and future—a view subsequent directors and critics have adopted. In France, Barrault's view that Chekhov had shown maximum economy in representation—"Not a single thing can be crossed out"—accredited *The Cherry Orchard* as a play that met all the criteria of art set by Racine and Flaubert. Chekhov was naturalized. France could now accept a Russian writer so un-Dostoyevskian, and the perfection of the play led critics to doubt that it should be subjected to the inevitable imperfections of production. Only the visit of the Moscow Arts Theater in 1958 with *The Cherry Orchard* sobered susceptible audiences into a pedestrian, Soviet-oriented view of Chekhov and his theater as faithful reproducers of reality and a herald of a brighter future.

By the 1950s, all over the Western world and in Japan, where overtones of *Macbeth* and the symbolism of the cherry blossom were particularly appreciated, *The Cherry Orchard* was established as a classic. Criticism was now concerned with providing guidance for correct interpretation. As modern structuralist brains drained from Prague to Boston, Paris, and Oxford, attention was paid to the integrity of Chekhov's text, casting the mold in which this study is set. The significance of every detail in the play—from the breaking string to the Duniasha's saucer, from traditional farce such as the dialogue of the deaf to the new absurdities of extraneous imagery (e.g., fish and billiards)—challenges critics to resolve the overall equivocations, to "make the silences resound" as Barrault put it. Research in Russia has established how manifold Chekhov's sources were, so that the very texture of the play seems as much a collage of phrases read and overheard as a linearly composed narrative. The new release of material from archives will uncover more sources for the raw material of the play. Questions of genre also preoccupy critics in Russia and abroad: In what sense can a play about the loss of property, love, and death be termed a "comedy," and is the answer in the play's formal structure rather than in the audience's stock responses to these losses?

Today, as new and antagonistic schools of criticism—whether feminist or deconstructionist—proliferate rapidly, *The Cherry Orchard* has been spared the gutting that other modern "classics" have undergone. But some recent productions of the play amount to a deconstructionist critical reception. Russian directors, once the thaw permitted dissent from official practices, rebelled against leisurely productions by the Moscow Arts Theater (its performance of *The Cherry Orchard* in Poland allegedly lasted five hours). Anatoli Efros's production in 1975 at Moscow's Taganka Theater, then the nearest to a radical theater in the Soviet Union, stretched neurosis in the characterization and morbidity in the sets to give an expressionist hysteria to Lopakhin and Ranevskaia and to create an atmosphere of funereal gloom. Efros's follower, Leonid Trushkin, produced a "cooperative" *Cherry Orchard* in 1990, where the "much esteemed bookcase" of act 1 becomes the whole set, turning the actors into marionettelike automata: against this background Ranevskaia appears as an Edith Piaf–like amoral life force, undefeated by the loss of the estate, filling the finale with comic optimism. In the October 1992 Moscow Festival, foreign *Cherry Orchard*s returned to Moscow to bewilder the Russians with German expressionism (Peter Stain) or Czech hysteria (Otomar Krejčí).

Recent non-Russian productions have translated not just the text but the whole setting. There have been Irish and even confederate American *Cherry Orchard*s (one being *The Wisteria Trees*, with black Dunia and Yasha; another Michael Schultz's all-black cast), although few spectators found universality unlocked by such transformations. Trevor Griffiths in Britain rewrote the text in order to give the play a neo-Trotskyist political analysis, a transformation so radical that it implies Chekhov's original play to be irrelevant to modern audiences. Peter Brook's 1981 Paris production sought universality by using an international cast, so that Chekhov was performed in French with English, Danish, and other accents, and almost no props, ridding the play of its Russianness. Trying "to play the myth—the secret play" was a high price paid to make Everyman and Everywoman protagonists of the play. The flight from Chekhov's explicit settings and dynamics and from the Moscow Art Theater's heritage led to an unfortunately unforgettable American interpretation of 1985: Joel Gersmann reduced the play to "They buy the farm, they lose the farm," kept only the theory of time zones (future shock and derelict past) from critical tradition, and subjected what was left to transvestism, punk rock, and violence, with Ranevskaia wielding a chainsaw, Trofimov having sexual intercourse with Ania on a stage free from props. Gersmann's sole achievement in "playing the subtext" was to use song to bring out the significance for what happens onstage to Ranevskaia's drowned son, Grisha: "Grisha's dead, Grisha's dead / Drowned in the river, No-one heard his screams."

Just as in classical music, the critical pendulum, however, has swung back in favor of observing the composer's original dynamics and even using period instruments to reconstruct original performances. Thus, in performing Chekhov, where we have to hand a body of interpretative guidance from the author and his first directors, the most powerful contemporary Russian productions, such as Vladimir Pakhomov's in the Lipetsk Theater, have reverted to a modified Stanislavskian interpretation, trusting the original text to bridge the increasing distance between us and Chekhov's times and using the archival and interpretative discoveries of Chekhov critics only where one might reasonably imagine the ghost of the author approving. In the West the publication of new translations, notably Michael Frayn's, where the language works onstage and is yet a professional rendering of Chekhov's Russian, has saved innovative directors coping with quaint, unintelligible, and unspeakable lines but at the same time deprived them of a pretext for radical misinterpretation.

A READING

4

The Making of the Text

It is not widely known that Chekhov had a cherry orchard of his own.
The first phrase crossed out in his notebooks for 1897 is just "cherry
orchard," and since the idea of the play and its title was not born until
1902, this refers to the 50 Vladimir cherry trees he planted on his
newly acquired estate at Melikhovo in 1892. Those trees were among
the timber chopped down in 1899 by a timber dealer called Konshin,
the purchaser of Melikhovo. The play thus has a poignant biographical link that sheds light on the characterization of Lopakhin, who buys
the cherry orchard. Despite destroying the trees Chekhov had planted,
Konshin found himself unable to pay more than his 25 percent deposit
on Chekhov's old estate, and in 1903 he lost it to a second purchaser.[1]

In fact, cherry orchards go back to Chekhov's childhood memories of southern Russia before the deforestations of the 1880s: the play
has a longer germination than anything Chekhov ever wrote. As a
child Chekhov spent holidays in the Ukraine, on Ragozina Balka, the
Donets farm of the Kravtsovs, known for its cherry orchard. "Steppe,"
a narrative that established Chekhov's rank in 1888, uses the author's
memories to convey the experience of Egorushka, a nine-year-old boy
crossing the Ukraine on a long summer journey. In chapter 1 the first

sights as the boy leaves town prefigure two elements in *The Cherry Orchard*, the graveyard and the cherry trees:

> The boy gazed at familiar places while the hateful carriage ran past and left everything behind. After the prison the black, soot-stained smithies flashed past, then the cosy, green cemetery, walled in by cobblestones; you could see cheerful white crosses and headstones over the wall, they were hidden in the greenery of the cherry trees and in the distance they seemed like white spots. Egorushka recalled that when the cherries flowered, these spots of white merged with the cherry blossom and became a sea of white; and when the cherries ripened, the white headstones and crosses would be spattered with spots as scarlet as blood. All day and all night Egorushka's father and grandmother slept under those cherry trees behind the cemetery wall.[2]

Thus an oriental association of cherry blossom with death and memory persists 16 years, from Chekhov's early masterpiece until his last play.

A letter from Vladimir Nemirovich-Danchenko to Chekhov, written in 1891 before the Moscow Arts Theater existed, when Nemirovich-Danchenko was just an actor, friend, and fellow southerner, challenges Chekhov to evoke a cherry orchard. Nemirovich-Danchenko was staying on his Ukrainian estate, Neskuchnoe, in Ekaterinoslav province. He wrote, "I could remind you of a delightful sultry midday, when there is such silence in the air, that you would think that the Mother of God had sent a blessing from above (I'm quoting from something), especially if you look at the dark cherry orchard. You ought to try, in fact, choosing the densest colors you can."[3]

The visual aspect of the play is undoubtedly influenced by painting as well as memories. Chekhov's study in his estate at Yalta had no fewer than five paintings by his friend the melancholic Isaak Levitan, whose penchant for moonlit fields, reflected in *A Haystack in a Moonlit Night*, inspired the moonlight in Chekhov's 1898 story "A Visit to Friends" and in act 2 of *The Cherry Orchard* (to which Stanislavsky added hay).

The theme of the estate on the verge of bankruptcy, however, is quite conventional: Chekhov's first and untitled play, hitherto known as *Platonov*,[4] has the same basic situation. Since the 1860s, when improvident Russian landowners first felt the risks of the new market economy, the predecessors of Ranevskaia and Gaev had become the stock in trade of a number of Russian novelists. Chekhov knew not only fictional examples but real ones: as the émigré novelist Mark Aldanov put it, when attacking Ivan Bunin for dismissing the realism of Chekhov's drama, "Chekhov had spent a lot of time on landowners' estates (e.g., the Kiseliovs at Babkino). Anyway, he knew far more Russian landowners than Bunin knew American millionaires."[5] The Kiseliovs, whom Chekhov had known for 15 years, are a plausible source: Aleksei Sergeevich Kiseliov unwittingly created the roles of Gaev and the aunt in Iaroslavl when he wrote to Chekhov in 1886, "Well, Chekhonte, tell me what to do. I've thought of one thing—I've set my authoress [his wife, Maria] to work writing a tearful letter to her aunt in Penza, saying, 'Save me, my husband and children.' . . . Perhaps she'll take pity and send not just enough to pay the 500 rubles but to buy us all some sweets. What can I tell you about myself? I'm getting fat, I eat and drink very well, sleep even better."[6] Maria Kiseliova had written in 1897 to tell Chekhov of their declining fortunes: "Babkino is largely falling apart, from the owners to the buildings . . . the owner has become an elderly infant, goodhearted and somewhat bruised."[7]

The Lintvariov estate at Sumy in the province of Kharkov, however, is geographically if not morally nearer the setting of *The Cherry Orchard*. Chekhov had spent two summer holidays (1888–89) as a guest there and his impressions of the neglected orchards in the area anticipate the atmosphere of the play: "Completely rundown, very poetic, sad estates where the souls of beautiful women live on."[8] Chekhov's first editor and patron, the once lowly Nikolai Leikin, had in 1885 bought an aristocrat's estate and boasted, like Lopakhin, to Chekhov, "Once noble counts owned it, and now it's me, Leikin, the oaf."[9] But Chekhov's neighbors at Melikhovo in the 1890s proliferated examples of estates lost by the fecklessness of charming, often expatriate owners; so do the advertisements for auctions and property sales in the Moscow press. The fantastic world of *The Cherry Orchard* is tightly tethered to prosaic reality. Perhaps uppermost in this final work of the dramatist are childhood memories, not just of cherry blossom but of his father's bankruptcy and of the distress purchase of the Chekhovs' house by the merchant and family friend whom they had thought their potential savior.

Chekhov usually burnt notes made on scraps of paper, even first drafts of his work: the fair copy of *The Cherry Orchard* is the only text he preserved. But his notebooks, particularly the first and largest, from the 1890s to his death, leave clues to the genesis of the text, although many of the entries are cryptic, practical and literary plans are inextricably entangled, and nearly all the initial ideas are completely transformed by the time they are incorporated into the finished work of art. Many ideas serve several works. The notebooks confirm that no Chekhov work can be understood in isolation: casual phrases such as his remark that Russian inns have "clean-smelling tablecloths"[10] echo in stories of the 1890s, such as "Three Years" or "His Wife," as well as in *The Cherry Orchard* (Ranevskaia remarks in act 2 that the table-cloths in the station restaurant "smelt of soap"). Often the most evocative, sensuous details that create the thick nonverbal atmosphere of *The Cherry Orchard* stem from impressions recorded in Chekhov's notebooks. Gaev's complaint to Yasha—"Who is it smelling of herring?"—stems from notes that "all the characters ask about N.: 'Why does he smell of dog?'" and "A character smells of fish and everyone tells him so" (*PPS*, 17: 75, 79). Chekhov recopied the best observations into a fourth notebook. Expressive samples of idiolect overheard or invented, such as Lopakhin's drunken "This is the fruit of your imagination, covered with the darkness of obscurity," were first recorded in the notebooks (*PPS*, 17: 43) sometimes a decade previously, as are pseudo-proverbs like Pishchik's "A hungry dog believes only in meat" (*PPS*, 17: 74) or Charlotta's "*Guter Mensch, aber schlechter Musikant*" (Nice man, but lousy musician; *PPS*, 17: 84).

The play's subplots weave together many disparate elements scattered through the notebooks. For instance, the theme of Ranevskaia's subconsciously conspiratorial efforts to marry off Varia and thus embroil Lopakhin (a theme much more dominant in "A Visit to Friends") goes back to notes for 1897 (*PPS*, 17: 76). The philosophizing speculations of the male characters are formulated later: in 1901 we have a speech that gives Trofimov's idealism in embryo: "In man only what our five senses can cope with dies, and what lies outside them, what is probably enormous, unimaginable, lofty and lies beyond our senses, remains alive" (*PPS*, 17: 85). 1902 sees a trickle of denunciation to be used both by Trofimov in *The Cherry Orchard* and by Sasha, the idealist provocateur, in the story "The Bride": "The estate has a nasty smell, a nasty tone; the trees are planted anyhow, absurdly; and in a far corner the watchman's wife is doing the guests' laundry all day and nobody can see her; and these gentry dare to talk for days on end about their rights, about decency. . . . [O]ur self-love and conceit are European, but our development and actions are Asiatic" (*PPS*, 17: 87).

Only in 1903 did Chekhov make Lopakhin a former serf of Gaev and decide on their surnames (*PPS*, 17: 84), but the theme of a nobleman losing his estate to a despised commoner is first noted in 1899 (*PPS*, 17: 70): "There is no trace of the old estate, all that is left is a lilac bush that unaccountably does not flower" (*PPS*, 17: 76). 1899 was a year particularly rich in details that were to be used in *The Cherry Orchard*. It was then that the character of Ranevskaia is born: "For a play: a liberal old woman dresses young, smokes, can't do without society, is attractive [*simpatichna*]." Her villa near Menton and the link to Kharkov is outlined: "A gentleman owns a villa near Menton that he bought with the money from selling an estate in Tula province. I saw him lose this villa at cards in Kharkov, where he was on business, then he had a job on the railways and died" (*PPS*, 17: 79). The impecunious Pishchik emerges at the same time: "In the first act X, a decent man, borrows 100 rubles from N. and for four acts does not return them" (*PPS*, 17: 77). This character's reliance on his daughter's lottery ticket is reflected in this 1902 comment: "A Russian's only hope is to win two hundred thousand" (*PPS*, 17: 87). When the character of Varia first surfaces (*PPS*, 17: 83) she is given the surname Nedotiopina, incorporating Firs's recurrent word of contempt, *nedotiopa* ("clumsy idiot") ("sillybilly" in Michael Frayn's version).[11] Charlotta's dog that allegedly eats nuts had a forebear in the note ("she fed her dog on real caviar" (*PPS*, 17: 87). Notes for 1903 show that the "deeply respected" bookcase whose centenary Gaev celebrates was one of the last elements to be invented: "Papers prove that bookcase has stood in the office for a hundred years; the officials in all seriousness celebrate its jubilee" (*PPS*, 17: 96).

The notebooks are just as informative about what Chekhov decided to omit: in act 4 Lopakhin was not only to hack down the cherry orchard but to surround it with notices: "unauthorized entry forbidden," "do not trample on the flowers." In the third notebook Iasha and Firs seem to refer to their master spending hours fishing, a subtext of *The Seagull*.

Memoirs of contemporaries are a richer but less reliable source of information about the making of the play. Stanislavsky's memoirs, which call for corroboration, are rich in recalled conversations with Chekhov, relevant to the making of *The Cherry Orchard*. One conversation he dates to the autumn of 1901 at the Moscow Arts Theater: "Chekhov started dropping a few hints on the plot of his next play. He fancied a wide-open window, with a branch of white cherry blossom, pushing into the room from the orchard. Then there was a room with people playing billiards."[12] Stanislavsky also recalled aborted ideas: the lady borrowing from her servant and the master staying in bed all day because his trousers were not ready. Stanislavsky claimed credit for introducing Chekhov to a real-life original of Charlotta— the English governess of his relatives, the Smirnovs, Lily Glassby. But research by Harvey Pitcher shows how Stanislavsky exaggerates: Lily and Charlotta share only being foreign waifs, speaking their minds wittily in fluent but unidiomatic Russian.[13] Charlotta's tricks, such as her ventriloqual crying baby, were in fact part of Olga Knipper's repertoire.

A play is more than phrases, themes, and characters. This play's origins lie in the Moscow Arts Theater and the pressure Stanislavsky and Nemirovich-Danchenko were putting on Chekhov in 1901 to add to their repertoire and to capitalize on the success of *Three Sisters*; they also lie in that peculiar fascination and antagonism that Chekhov felt for theater as a genre, an interface with the public, a relationship that mirrors his friendships and affairs with actresses. One of the purposes of a new play was to thwart expectations, to puzzle performers, to provoke. *The Cherry Orchard* has a genesis independent of its commissioning or the material that had accumulated for it.

The Making of the Text

In April 1901 Chekhov told his wife, "I have moments when I feel a very strong desire to write a four-act vaudeville or comedy for the Moscow Arts Theater. And I will, if nothing stops me, only I shan't submit it before the end of 1903."[14] The comic instinct was dominant: "I dream of writing a funny play with the devil causing chaos." The play itself was conceived in January 1902, when a letter to Olga Knipper talks of a play "that has just flickered in my brain, like the first break of dawn" (No. 3633). A list of characters was compiled by June 1902, but Chekhov still hedged coquettishly. He wrote to Stanislavsky, before spending the summer fishing at the director's dacha, Liubimovka, "If I begin a play," and he wrote three times in August and September to Knipper saying that he would not (Nos. 3801, 3814, 3831). Only in October, when autumn had brought back his tubercular cough, did he surrender to Stanislavsky: "I have a plot, but not enough gunpowder yet" (No. 3854). By December, spurred on perhaps by the perpetual need to earn money, he was promising to write from morning till night. The play was now referred to by its title.

Maria Chekhova recalls a day in Yalta, perhaps in the autumn of 1902: "Suddenly he takes a little piece of paper, writes on it and his eyes creased in a smile, shows it to me. I read *The Cherry Orchard*. To my look of enquiry, my brother replies, 'That's going to be the name of my new play.'"[15] The decision on the play's title is striking. Chekhov took little interest in his titles: they were unadventurous and sometimes ephemeral. Who else could have entitled a work "A Dreary Story" or named a whole succession of plays from *Ivanov* to *Uncle Vania* after the male protagonist? *The Cherry Orchard* is far subtler in Russian, for, talking to Stanislavsky, Chekhov decided that it would not be the normal designation *Víshnevy sad*, with the stress on the *i*, but *Vishnióvy sad*—the owners' affected pronunciation hinting that the orchard was abnormal, uncommercial.[16]

Despite the serendipity of the title, however, Chekhov's letters from Yalta to his wife in Moscow show that few texts gave him as much torment as *The Cherry Orchard*. Its action was at first compressed into three long acts instead of the usual four: "Though I don't care, because the play will be identical either way." As news of its composition spread, the pressure from actresses—not only from Olga

Knipper ("Will the cherry blossom open soon?" she kept asking)—became unrelenting. The great St. Petersburg actress Vera Komissarzhevskaia, then 38, begged to have the St. Petersburg performance rights and presumably the lead part. Chekhov tried to deter her. Here is what he wrote to her: "1) True, the play is planned, and I have a title (*The Cherry Orchard* but that's a secret for the time being) and I shall get down to writing it probably no later than February [1903], if of course I am well enough. 2) The central role in this play is an old woman!!—to the author's regret, and 3) if I offer the play to the Arts theater, then, according to its terms, it will have exclusive rights to the play" (No. 3981). Recovering from a bout of pleurisy, working in a freezing study, in a snowbound Crimean February, Chekhov (in a letter to Stanislavsky) envisaged the play's whiteness: "Act 1, cherry blossom seen through the windows, an utterly white orchard. And the ladies in white dresses" (No. 3990). Like his heroine, he longed to get away to Western Europe: completing the play that spring became urgent. Perhaps this quickened the dramatic tempo, and accounts for the insistence on laughter, on the comic nature of Knipper's part (at first Varia) and Stanislavsky's (Gaev). Only the main part (presumably Ranevskaia's) would not crystalize. By March Chekhov was cutting the number of characters to make the play "more intimate."

Even after the play was written Chekhov referred to his erotically charged heroine as "the old woman," which seems to show a change from his original conception of a foolish old woman losing her estate. As Chekhov's bisexual admirer, the novelist Tatiana Shchepkina-Kupernik recalls, in 1903 "his heroine kept getting younger until she reached such a stage that Olga Knipper need not hesitate playing her."[17] Yet in December 1902, still calling his heroine "the old woman," Chekhov was assigning the part to the actress Anna Azagarova (not employed by the Moscow Arts Theater), who was only in her forties. In April 1903, however, he still insisted to his wife that the theater would need "an actress for the part of a lady who's getting on in years [*pozhilaia*], otherwise there'll be no play" (No. 4063). When Knipper asked for the part herself, Chekhov objected that he had already cast her and that she had once played "an old lady in *The*

Seagull"—a remark that shows that Chekhov considered his heroine old in her mid-forties.

That month Chekhov escaped from the Crimea, where illness had confined him; had his despair about his health confirmed in Moscow; and, accompanied by his wife, continued *The Cherry Orchard* at Naro-Fominsk, on an estate 40 miles southwest of Moscow. That summer he toured estates for sale, making a last desultory attempt to buy another country house for himself. Submission of *The Cherry Orchard* was postponed until October. By August he was back in the Crimea. The setting of the play was contracted. "I've reduced the production side of the play to the minimum, no special sets will be needed and you won't have to invent any new gunpowder" (No. 4156), he assured Nemirovich-Danchenko in late August, which contradicted other instructions. "I've put in instead an old wayside shrine and a well. That's more peaceful. But in act 2 you must give me a real green field and a road and a distance that is unusual on stage." Act 2, he complained in his next letter to Nemirovich-Danchenko (No. 4162), was causing trouble: by now he was reconciled to Olga (who had put on weight) playing the part of the "mother" (no longer the "old woman"), while Maria Lilina, Stanislavsky's wife, was now to take on Varia. He begins to stress the subtitle "comedy." Now our problems, and those of Stanislavsky's cast begin, for Chekhov never retracted the mischievous assertion of September 1903: "The last act will be cheerful, and the whole play cheerful and frivolous" (No. 4166). The letters to Knipper go on: "The fourth act of my play, compared with the other acts, will be thin in content, but effective. The finale of your part seems pretty good to me" (No. 4177). A shy pride emerges: "I think that there is something new in my play, however boring it may be. There is not a single shot in the play, by the way" (No. 4177).

By 26 September the draft was complete, and Chekhov slowly began revising it, sometimes only a line or two a day, for the fair copy. With Maria's departure for Moscow, the cook in the Yalta household ignored Chekhov's diet: the resulting stomach complications made the play seem "immeasurably enormous, colossal, I'm horrified and have lost all appetite for it" (No. 4188). As the play neared completion in an appropriately deserted house, the specter of the censor and his spoiling pen appeared. A new fair copy was begun. Finally, on 14 October, the only copy of the play was dispatched in confidence to Knipper for the theater, together with a reply-paid envelope and a request for a telegram of acceptance. Accompanying instructions show what a strong feeling of paternity Chekhov had for this play:

> 1) You are to play Liubov [Ranevskaia], for there's nobody else. She is dressed with great taste, but not expensively. She's clever, very kind, absent-minded; she's affectionate to everyone, always a smile on her face. 2) A nice young actress must play Ania. 3) Varia's part might be taken by Maria Petrovna [Lilina]. 4) Gaev is for Vishnevsky. Ask Vishnevsky to listen to people playing billiards and note as many billiard terms as he can. I don't play billiards, rather I used to, but have forgotten it all, and it's all haphazard in my play. Then Vishnevsky and I will discuss it and I'll write whatever is needed. 5) Lopakhin is Stanislavsky. 6) Trofimov, the student, is Kachalov. 7) Simeonov-Pishchik is Gribunin. 8) Charlotta is a question mark. I shall insert more words in act 4. . . . In act 4 Charlotta will perform a trick with Trofimov's galoshes. Raevskaia can't do it. You need an actress with a sense of humor. . . . The house is an old nobleman's house; people used to live a very wealthy life there, and this must be brought out in the production. Wealthy and comfortable. Varia is rough and a little dim, but very kind. (No. 4199)

As the play entered rehearsal, Chekhov's letter fought any tearful interpretation: "Why," he asked Nemirovich-Danchenko, "do you telegraph me to say there is a lot of weeping in the play? Where are these weeping people? Just Varia, but that's because she is a cry-baby by nature, and her tears must not make the spectator sad. I often write *on the verge of tears*, but that shows a person's mood, not real tears" (No. 4213). Even his wife's interpretation of the lead part had to be wrestled with: "No, I never wanted to make Ranevskaia settle down. Only death can settle a woman like her. . . . It's not hard to play Ranevskaia, you just have to get the tone right straight away; you have to find a smile and a way of laughing, to know how to dress. . . . Don't learn your part too thoroughly, you'll need to consult me more; and don't order any dresses until I come" (Nos. 4215, 4233). Knipper had reacted inappropriately to the manuscript in her telegrams of congratulations (15 and 18 October 1903): "In the fourth act I burst out sobbing."

Chekhov failed to get his way over most of the casting. When Stanislavsky appropriated the part of Gaev and left Lopakhin for Leonidov, Chekhov was upset: "Lopakhin's part is central. If it doesn't succeed, the whole play will fail" (No. 4221); "Lopakhin mustn't be acted by a shouter, he mustn't be a merchant: he is a soft person" (No. 4224). Despite Chekhov's warning that Leonidov would make Lopakhin a *kulachok* (a tight-fisted peasant exploiter), Stanislavsky was obdurate. Chekhov also feared that theater intrigues would let unsuitable actresses get parts he had not intended for them.[18] Only over the part of Ranevskaia, played by his wife, did Chekhov have full control: while she had a mind of her own and could be obtuse, her interpretation is probably authorial. Knipper-Chekhova recalled to her biographer, M. Turovskaia, "When I was preparing the part of Ranevskaia, I thought, 'Why does everything fall apart in her hands?' . . . She has an inner disorientation, spiritual restlessness [*neprikaiannost'*]."[19] Because the director, Stanislavsky, had decided to play Gaev rather than Lopakhin, the play's center of gravity was shifting against Chekhov's intentions and toward the doomed gentry, rather than the forces that oust them.

Never before had Chekhov attached so much importance to the theatre's choice of performer for each role. Even discounting a dying man's irritability (which we see in his letters to his wife and to Stanislavsky between the play's completion and its first performance), we get the impression of a perfectionist for whom his new play deviates from his own canon—a work that cannot be produced without guidance by the author. Similarities in characterization were misleading: Ania was not a reincarnation of Irina in *Three Sisters*, nor was Varia a variant of Sonia in *Uncle Vania*. As we shall see, never had Chekhov visualized characters so graphically. Too ill to leave the Crimea, he became furstrated as the Moscow theater ignored half his recommended casting. He was embarrassed to find that he had effectively promised the text to two rival publishers—the radical Znanie house led by his rival Maksim Gorky[20] and Marks, the publisher of his collected works. Garbled accounts of the plot of *The Cherry Orchard* leaked to newspapers infuriated him. He suspected his stage directions were ignored, that his "drawing room" (*gostinaia*) had been replaced by a hotel (*gostinitsa*) (Nos. 4227, 4228). In one letter he told Stanislavsky that he trusted him to design sets "a hundred times better than I could have thought up"; in another the director had to be reminded that the play took place in a big old stone or wooden house, with solid, classic, antique furniture. Typically precise in rural matters, Chekhov protested that the director's act 2 special effects were nonsense: there could be no noises of corncrakes or frogs at haymaking time. Stanislavsky's fondness for passing trains backstage was equally irritating (No. 4248).

Chekhov transferred his trust to Nemirovich-Danchenko and complained by letter and telegram about casting: "For three years I've been preparing to write *The Cherry Orchard*, and for three years I've been telling you to invite an actress for the part of Ranevskaia. So now you have effectively set out a game of patience that will never come out" (No. 4224). To Chekhov's annoyance, Olga Knipper encouraged the Tolstoyan radical L. A. Sulerzhitsky to think he had some affinity with Trofimov. Chekhov disabused him of this notion: "Trofimov doesn't resemble you in the least. . . . My play is fated—it began with misunderstandings and it will end with misunderstandings" (No. 4224), he concluded by the end of November. In early December he left for Moscow to rejoin his text. While Stanislavsky appreciated (as his notes prove, when we study them in conjunction with the play) the "lacelike" lightness of texture and "watercolor" impressionism of Chekhov's text, reports of the rehearsals imply that this appreciation was a long time crystalizing. Nemirovich-Danchenko, in a 1908 letter to N. E. Efros, confessed that it took four more years' production before the "heavy, cumbersome drama" became a "lacelike gracious picture."[21] Chekhov's reactions at rehearsal were irritable to the point of perversity, contradicting his own stage directions when he asks Lopakhin not to shout, retorting "Well!" when an actor asked for guidance on how to play a part. By Christmas, Stanislavsky had to persuade Chekhov to stay away. Stanislavsky wrote to the actress V. V. Kotliarevskaia, "The orchard is not yet blossoming. No sooner had the first flowers appeared than the author came and confused us all. The flowers have fallen and only now do we have new buds."[22] By December 1903 the text itself was through the censors and out of Chekhov's hands, in the theater's and publishers' control, and many cuts and alterations were irreversible.

The fair copy that survives in the manuscript section of the Russian State Library is the text Chekhov dispatched to Moscow on 14 October 1903. It was then typed up (carelessly) for submission to the state censors. When Chekhov arrived he incorporated into the manuscript (as interlinear insertions) new passages to patch the cuts made in Trofimov's denunciatory speeches by the censor. (These cuts were left in the manuscript in brackets, and only in editions and translations since 1932 have they been restored.) Once he saw how actors disfigured his conceptions, Chekhov rewrote certain parts, particularly Lopakhin's. To prevent a crude, one-sided interpretation, he gave Lopakhin more words of affection, and in compensation he made Gaev more absurd and irritating. The cuts that Stanislavsky forced on act 2, however, removing the final scenes and altering part of the servants' dialogue, were so radical that Chekhov had to copy the whole act separately. The surviving manuscript on stiff white paper is impressive in its economy: there are no left- or right-hand margins, no hyphenation; the writing, clear and firm, has no flourishes. The play was written slowly, in short bursts, conserving the author's ebbing vitality. Great precision is everywhere: the word *nedotiopa* has its stress and pronunciation indicated; the handwriting flows faster in the long speeches of Ranevskaia and is most abrupt in the servants' dialogues of act 2, which suggests the relative ease of the passionate tirade and the elusiveness of the comedy of the absurd and the irrelevant.

Chekhov's last literary work in January and February 1904 was further revision of the text in correcting the proofs for the Znanie edition of *The Cherry Orchard* (which did not appear until May of that year). Stage directions, especially those indicating tone and mood, are still more precise; Lopakhin is made still more sensitive (he now smiles kindly when he picks up Varia's keys); Trofimov is given unexpected lines of affection toward his antagonist ("You have fine, tender fingers, like an artist's, you have a fine, tender soul"). For many years, however, the Moscow Arts Theater persisted with a text that incorporates other changes, including the actor Ivan Moskvin's additions to his part of Epikhodov, and Chekhov's death prevented a final, unified text ever being drafted.

In today's world *The Cherry Orchard* is more often performed in translation than in the original Russian. It is beyond the scope of this study to discuss the history of its translation into dozens of languages, but the history and problems of its translation into English parallel Gaev's remark in act 1: "If a disease has many treatments, then it must be incurable." "If a text has many translations, then it must be untranslatable." Some 20 translations have been published in the last 80 years: the problem is insoluble. The nature of translation is partly responsible: Chekhov's 1903 Russian cannot be rendered by later translators into 1903 English, and each generation will require a version in its own literary language. Translation demands neutrality of tone—nothing specifically asynchronic with Chekhov's time or the reader's time—which makes for blandness. There are conflicting schools of translation, from one extreme—the literal "Byzantine" school that demands that the original, should it ever be lost, be fully recoverable from the translation—to the other—which aims to present the audience with what would have been written had Chekhov and his cast been born and bred abroad.

In drama, as in song and opera, the text must be performable and work both in the mouths of actors and onstage. The early English translations by Calderon and Garnett suffered because neither knew what worked onstage and neither had mastered the Russian language. Later translators, such as Marian Fell, were no better, or, like Elizaveta Fen, had a native competence in Russian unmatched by unidiomatic English. As a result, versions grew out of imperfect collaboration between a translator who knew what the Russian meant and a director who knew what he wanted his actors to say—more adaptations than translations. Recently translation has become more professional. Ronald Hingley's Oxford Chekhov gives a text that does not misrepresent the original and is literary English. Nevertheless, it is not easily performable, and preference is now given to Michael Frayn's 1978 (revised 1988) Methuen version. As Frayn is a professional dramatist with interpreter-standard Russian, he is unlikely to be superseded in his time as a translator of *The Cherry Orchard*. Nevertheless, his stage sense has forced him to take drastic measures where the Russian means more to a native than to a foreign audience, and a full discussion of the play sometimes requires literal translation and exegesis.

From inception to first performance, the three years' evolution of the text of *The Cherry Orchard* shows a complex interaction of the theater with Chekhov's intentions. The decisive element in the genesis of *The Cherry Orchard*, however, is to be found in literature—in Chekhov's reading of others' work and in his rereading of his own. In Chekhov's earlier work and in his reading of classical and contemporary Russian and European literature we find the literary genomes that shaped this play. Most of Chekhov's time in the last four years of his life was spent selecting and revising his work for republication in his collected works: this proves how prominent his earlier work was in composing his last pieces. Similarly, the fame of his last years made him a natural choice as reader and reviewer for new work and new translations: his exposure to other authors, especially to contemporaries, had never been greater.

One speculation might be ventured: that the theme and characters of Chekhov's last play paralleled the last years of his life. While all his plays (except *Ivanov*) are built around the disruption of a stagnant household living with its ghosts, by the irruption of destructively dynamic outsiders, and thus superficially resemble Chekhov's family life at Melikhovo and Yalta, his last years were especially clouded by conflict between his wife and sister. A struggle between the newcomer and the established housekeeper for recognition, it was also a conflict between the staid Lutheran Olga Knipper (whom Chekhov originally cast as the would-be nun Varia) and the assertive, sexually liberated Maria Chekhova. Rivalry between two women for command of the household is the comedy of *Uncle Vania* and part of the drama of *Three Sisters*. In *The Cherry Orchard* the disparity of the passionately involved Ranevskaia with her innocent, naive, and sexless household and the comments that her brother makes about her "depraved" nature echo the letters (unpublished) that Chekhov was receiving from his elder brother Aleksandr Pavlovich, urging him to be forbearing about Maria's active love life and defending her against the strictures of Olga Knipper, who wanted her "expelled from the house for misusing her 'cactus' [apparently slang for genitalia] with a married man, unknown to me." Aleksandr Pavlovich in fact affected the composition of Chekhov's dialogue, not excluding *The Cherry Orchard*. He reminded Chekhov of the southern Russian and foreign speech peculiarities and phrases they had heard as schoolboys in Taganrog. For instance, Pishchik's exclamation of amazement in act 1, "I'll throw caution to the wind" (literally, "Let my carriage be wrecked, all four wheels"), comes from Aleksandr's witty and subversive eight-page letter of November 1903.[23] Chekhov's dramatic language draws on his family's speech and his subject material on their conflicts, but the process by which this raw material was refined is so mysterious that we cannot determine how accidental or significant are the common features.

5

Act 1

The Cherry Orchard can best be understood by reading it as the culmination of all Chekhov's major plays, particularly of the two preceding, *The Seagull* (1896) and *Three Sisters* (1901), which share many similarities in theme and structure. More important still is the fact that Chekhov the playwright is inseparable from Chekhov the story writer, and a full understanding of *The Cherry Orchard* is only possible when we see how he refers to, and reuses, the material of his stories. "A Visit to Friends" (1898), for example, is very close in its treatment of the theme of the improvident family about to lose their estate. Earlier stories, especially those set in the south of Russia, likewise deal with the destruction of nature in general or an orchard in particular, and they introduce many of the effects and symbols of *The Cherry Orchard*. In the chapters of this section I explore fully this play's links to such stories as "Panpipes" (1887), "The Black Monk" (1895), and "The Bride" (1903).

An audience's first impressions of a play often come in the hurried minutes spent studying the program notes: the subtitle "Comedy in Four Acts" sets expectations of mood, tempo, duration, and resolution that the play is to tease until its end. The next information sought by every audience is the cast list, in which they match characters to actors and try to establish in advance the relationship between the parts. Here, too, Chekhov teases them, for the usual symmetry of male and female has gone: the leading three roles are female, and all but one male part—Gaev's—are peripheral to the central family group, itself ominously outnumbered by servants and visitors. Yet the audience is immediately tempted to read into the presence of two girls, Ania and Varia, and two outside males, Lopakhin and Trofimov, a typical comic plot of couples surmounting obstacles to marriage—another source of expectations by which Chekhov turns the comedy against the audience. Those familiar with Chekhovian drama will search in vain for the character of the doctor, whose absence is one of the most ominous elements in the play. The Serbian critic Jovan Hristič sees the cast structure as a Copernican one, in which the main characters are planets revolving around a sun. This center of gravity is not a character but the orchard itself. If the orchard is the sun and the characters are planets revolving around it, then Gaev and Ranevskaia are the nearest and most affected by the orchard's gravitational power, while Trofimov and Pishchik are the farthest and the least affected. Although, as Hristič points out, all Chekhov's plays after *Ivanov* gravitate around a symbol, *The Cherry Orchard* is "the most democratic" of plays with no central human protagonist.[1]

The surnames of characters also give some clue to their character: from Fonvizin to Ostrovsky the flaws and virtues of the characters are hinted in their names. Chekhov usually refuses to give such hints: his earlier plays rely on the most neutral, even banal names (Ivanov is the Russian equivalent of Johnson). While some English-speaking critics have searched for associations, such as Gaev from *gaer* (clown), these associations are unconvincing and irrelevant. Lopakhin might suggest the root *lop-* in the words "to burst" (*lopnut'*) or "spade" (*lopata*), but Chekhov would have found funnier ways to suggest explosiveness or crudity. Chekhov does suggest tension between Lopakhin's present social status—that of an up-and-coming businessman—and his humble roots: his Christian name Ermolai is ineradicably rustic.[2] Even if Ranevskaia's perfectly normal Christian name

Act 1

Liubov' (love) signals her erotic drive, I doubt whether the surnames carry much semantic weight. True, the Gogolian name Simeonov-Pishchik (Pishchik means "squeaker") tells us that this is a caricature, not a character. Certainly the name Epikhodov, with its mixed Greek-Russian etymology of *epi* (about) and *khod-* (walk), suggests his characteristic perambulation, his ubiquity in the play wherever he is unwanted.

The servants' names also give the audience advance information: Duniasha and Iasha are both affectionate diminutives for Avdotia and Iakov, respectively. This implies the servants feel relaxed with their masters in this household. The name Firs, however, strikes a different resonance: the Russian version of the Greek Thyrses, it was a pastoral, pseudo-classical name that an eighteenth-century landowner would have found amusing to bestow on a serf. It bespeaks Firs's great age and anachronistic loyalties. It gives Firs a symbolic role of Time Past, the spirit of Antiquity by which the present can be assessed.

The only substantial contemporary Russian comment, however, on Chekhov's names was from Ivan Bunin, who dismissed the surname Ranevskaia (like the name Zarechnaia in *The Seagull*) as the sort of name not to be found among the gentry but a pseudonym a provincial actress would choose. If Bunin is right, then perhaps Chekhov intended Ranevskaia to be in name as well as person, like Zarechnaia, an actress, a *poseuse*. It is certainly ironic that the very real Russian actress Faina Ranevskaia was just eight years old when Chekhov created her namesake.

Once the curtain rises, the audience's experience differs from the readers. Chekhov the story writer cannot help giving the reader information he withholds from the spectator. Minutes pass before the spectator realizes that the set of act 1 is a room still called the nursery, that Ania's room leads off it. That it is dawn, not dusk; that the white blossom in the window is that of the cherry trees; and that the girl and the merchant who are so well-dressed are in fact the lowly Duniasha and the once lowly Lopakhin is only gradually revealed to the spectator. Stanislavsky's initial production notes (which have additions in Nemirovich-Danchenko's hand) show that his sets did everything possible to give the audience a substitute for a textual description of the setting: his stage is dimly lit by skylights, while shutters blank off the back. In his mania for detail Stanislavsky demanded the chugging and whistling of the train arriving, red light coming from a stove, a mouse-trap set in the corner of the room, candles guttering, a kennel full of dogs howling, and—for the entire play, reinforcing the imagery of dis-integration—squeaking floorboards, torn curtains, and chunks of falling plaster. To signal to the audience that Duniasha for all her fine clothes and delicate manners is a servant, Stanislavsky had her opening shutters, shutting the stove and wiping her nose on an apron. Similarly, Lopakhin's elegant dress ("white waistcoat, yellow suede shoes") and book in hand, as specified by Chekhov, are annulled by Stanislavsky having him enter disheveled, quietly cursing, smoking, spitting, picking his teeth with a match, wiping the mist from the win-dowpane and dusting a chair with his overcoat.

The reader will still note what even Stanislavsky's audience will miss: that the act is not broken down into scenes but flows in a continuum through exits and entrances.[3] Chekhov stopped dividing acts into scenes in *The Seagull* (1896), and the continuity of the act prompts us to compare his construction of a drama to that of a classi-cal symphony. In fact, others—notably Nemirovich-Danchenko and Meierkhold—had already compared the play to music. Their intuition is backed up when we analyze Chekhov's acts, for the form of act 1 can sensibly be construed as a sonata, with an exposition, a develop-ment through various keys, and a recapitulation of the exposition. Here the exposition seems conventional: two apparently secondary characters give a compressed synopsis to prepare the audience for the entry of the lead actress and establish a mood of joy, nostalgia, and anxiety. But the emphasis is typically Chekhovian, with six temporal references in the first half minute. Lopakhin's first question, "What's the time?," is the perpetual refrain and the theme of Chekhovian drama. We are not allowed to forget future dates and past anniver-saries, and, quite unlike other playwrights, Chekhov does not shy away from the fact that stage time and real time may differ in speed by a fac-tor of six or more; he continually emphasises the disparity, so that our watches seem to be horrendously slow and time on stage precipitously fast. (But note that the second function of Lopakhin's question is to show us that Duniasha the servant has bourgeois pretensions: she owns a watch.)

Duniasha's response to Lopakhin's question—2 A.M.—points out Chekhov's fondness for setting his action at times when the normal world is asleep (compare with act 3 of *Three Sisters* or act 2 of *Uncle Vania*). This setting presented a challenge to Stanislavsky at a time when the art of electric stage lighting was in its infancy: the sun or moon rising and setting are key elements in the conditioning of Chekhov's moods. The times of dawn and dusk also have other coordinating functions: they indicate the season. When the stage directions say "May," the spectator can only guess the season by the early hour of daybreak and the frost on the windowpanes, until Epikhodov enters to announce the temperature. The nursery in act 1, like act 4, when nobody has bothered to stoke the fires, is as cold as a castle in *Macbeth* (and in *Three Sisters* Chekhov specifically used the cold and the time of daybreak to indicate a semi-Arctic location).

Time, of course, is money, and it is natural that Lopakhin should be a chief source of numerical information, whether of dates, sums, or temperature. But as the exposition progresses the frequent references to time reveal that all the cast are prisoners of the past. Lopakhin first moves the time scale of the action back five years by mentioning that Ranevskaia has been abroad for that long and then further back (about 20 years) by recalling her cleaning up his bloody nose when he was 15. It also gives the first hint of Lopakhin's inner weakness or tenderness: Is he so fixated by adolescent gratitude to Ranevskaia that he will never fulfill Varia's expectations? (In Chekhov's original manuscript the bleeding nose incident occurred when Lopakhin was five or six.)

The originality of this opening "scene" in fact lies in the ambiguities Chekhov builds into Lopakhin and Duniasha, who give conflicting class signals. Lopakhin's white waistcoat signals gentrification, while his yellow shoes (yellow in Chekhov always suggests detestation and decay) signal vulgarity. Duniasha's mix of her mistress's cast-off dresses and a servant's apron is equally discordant. A new egalitarian dress code is implied by both their speech and the clothes Chekhov specifies (or "vestimentary markers," as modern critics term them). Chekhov in fact gives 35 indications of "vestimentary markers" in the play, identifying dress as an important nonverbal element. Clothes may make the man, but nothing and nobody is what it or he seems in *The Cherry Orchard*: Lopakhin's gentlemanly garb misleads us as much as Epikhodov's guitar that he claims to be a mandoline, or Charlotta's parcel that cries like a baby.

It is speech, however, that reveals character. A minute or two elapse before Lopakhin puts up the old class barriers by addressing Duniasha with the familiar *ty* (thou). Lopakhin may carry a book in his hand (that Stanislavsky has him tossing onto the nearest chair), but his Russian lapses now into a peasant's turn of phrase. He uses the word *vypivshi* (drunk) in reference to his father, and in telling off Duniasha he lapses into the tyrannical, curt pomposity traditionally associated with Russia's merchant classes, at least in their theatrical images: *Tak nel'zia. Nado sebia pomnit'* ("Not the way, is it? You want to remember who you are").

We are dealing with an aspect of Chekhov's genius that eludes translation: idiolect, the way in which a character's speech habits give away his class, his history, and his relationships (affection, parentage) with other speakers. Lopakhin's idiolect is the most diverse in the play: it can be abrupt or flowing, it embraces drunken abuse and educated philosophizing, it mirrors his association with peasants, merchants, the Ranevskaia-Gaev family, and even the intellectual Trofimov. Duniasha, like Epikhodov and Iasha, also speaks a bastard language, from the natural peasant *chuiut, chto khoziaeva edut* ("they can sense that the mistress is coming") to the standard genteel female's "I'm going to faint." Chekhov refines centuries of comic tradition in exploiting the servants' speech pretensions for laughs, but the phenomenon of idiolect is very subtly observed. While Duniasha oscillates between affected and natural poles, with "scene" 2 and Epikhodov's entry with a bunch of inappropriate flowers, we hear the comedy of the wrongly chosen word—the malapropism—with the humor of unintended obscenity and meaninglessness. Here the linguistic confusion is between the language of learned books, the whine of an ill-educated depressive, and the peremptory tones of an estate manager. Again we have a mélange beyond the scope of the best translator. "Allow me to communicate to you" ("And I mean look at me" in the Frayn version), says Epikhodov, using the unfortunate *prisovokupit'* ("to communicate"), which recalls *sovokupit'* ("to copulate").

Although the director's "squeaking floorboards" must have spoilt the effect of Epikhodov's "squeaking boots," Stanislavsky reinforces the farcical entry of Epikhodov with so much business that it is puzzling as to why Chekhov should ever have accused the Moscow Arts Theater of not reading the text, of making a tragedy out of it. Epikhodov was to drop the flowers because he was also trying to manage a hat and shake Duniasha's hand. He then wipes his nose with a handkerchief "as if playing a violin." The servants' "scene" ends in a typically Chekhovian cyclic recapitulation of Lopakhin's "five years" and Duniasha's fainting. The stage is empty for a time, before and after Firs enters, foreshadowing the play's last scene. Firs wears ancient livery and a top hat, a marker of his loyalties to a long-gone era, before emancipation disrupted social order. Like Chekhov's earlier half-senile servants—Marina in *Uncle Vania* or Anfisa and Ferapont in *Three Sisters*—Firs's decrepitude makes him an unexpected voice of skeptical sanity.

After Firs's portentous silent passage the main characters pass across the stage en masse in a sudden flurry of exclamations, with nobody responding to anybody else—the pathos of the homecoming is drowned in the "dialogue of the deaf." Only Ania's question, "Mama, do you remember?," gets an answer, which finally tells the spectators where they are: "The nursery." Stanislavsky intensified the pause before the mass entry by having two servants, Efimiushka and Polia (merely mentioned by Varia in Chekhov's text), creeping across the stage then hiding and watching. To spectators who had seen earlier Chekhov plays, the characters are easily guessable: Ania in innocent white (like Irina in *Three Sisters*) and Varia the would-be nun in black (like Sonia in *Uncle Vania* or the Mashas in *The Seagull* and *Three Sisters*). The imposing Paris-dressed Ranevskaia (Olga Knipper was a *roskoshnaia* [voluptuous], almost blowsy, woman) stands out, like Arkadina against Nina in *The Seagull*, from the slender monochrome girls, inverting the usual contrast of youth and age.

Like every act of the play, this one depends on a musical repetition of key words and phrases for its unity. The train being late "by two hours" is commented on by Gaev after Lopakhin; Ania comments on the "not sleeping" after Duniasha does; the theme of frost passes from the lips of Epikhodov to Varia to Duniasha. The chaotic arrival scene ends in apparent absurdity, with Charlotta's commenting that "My dog can eat nuts even." But even this casual invention is part of the fabric, for the theme of unusual food is to be developed a few minutes later with Ranevskaia's joke that she ate crocodile in Paris and with Pishchik swallowing all her pills. (The swallowing of pills, frog, and crocodile, like the contents of a witch's cauldron, is one of the first reminiscences of *Macbeth*.)

The next scene, in which Duniasha helps Ania to undress, makes act 1 a mirror image of act 4, wherein coats are put on and possessions gathered in the same room. (Stanislavsky understood this reversal well, for he had the characters in act 1 dump the galoshes and shoes that were to play such a part in act 4.) Ania barely listens to Duniasha: what strikes reader and spectator is the genetic link between her idiolect and her mother's. Both speak in ecstatic exclamations. Ranevskaia: "My own dear room, my lovely room. . . . I slept in here when I was a little girl." Ania: "My room, my windows, just as if I'd never been away." Repetition subtly reinforces the common characteristics and weaves a tighter dramatic fabric. These echoes also suggest the inability of the character—anticipating Samuel Beckett—to maintain an independent train of thought; his or her thoughts are also suddenly aborted by the physical objects he or she is encumbered with: "I've gradually lost all the [hair]pins," complains Ania, and in the next scene Varia's lament to Ania about her unrealized hopes of a proposal suddenly breaks off when she notices, "You've got a bumble-bee brooch."

In the middle of Ania's undressing comes the first hint of a ghost. For some reason Trofimov must be kept out: he is living in the bathhouse, that spidery wooden construction so redolent of evil in Russian literature. Ania's tone of joy clashes with the sullenness of Varia, whose bunch of keys ring out at every dangerous moment in the play. The mention of the unmentionable past releases a flow of information, so that the exposition now becomes complete. As if for the spectators' benefit, Ania tells Varia of the misery of Ranevskaia's life in Menton and Paris—although the existence of the lover, the living ghost of the play, is not yet explicit—and Ranevskaia, as a classic comic incarnation of a vice, is presented to us as a spendthrift rather than a debauchee. Varia's part in this exchange of information is to give the focal theme and time of the action—the family's failure to pay their debts and the auction of the estate set for August. We thus have a flow of time to a cut-off point, three months hence, typical of the structure of tragedy, and the unmanageable but banal vice of improvidence, typical of the stock in trade of comedy. It is a confusion of genre typical not just of Chekhov (the same progression of debt to financial crisis constitutes the plot of almost all his major drama) but of Russian drama from its inception in the 1760s (e.g., Fonvizin). Chekhov uses time, as does Racine, as a finite resource; but Chekhov's protagonists, unlike the heroines of classical tragedy, are less aware than the audience of time expiring.

In musical terms, the impending auction is the main theme of the play; the secondary theme, so typical of classical comedy, is the potential mating of eligible couples, and Varia's complaints "on the verge of tears" (*skvoz' sliozy*) are recognizably and traditionally the nearest classical comedy comes to pathos. We need only compare her distress with that of the heroines of Molière: the difference is, as always in Chekhov, that the audience will be thwarted of the traditionally happy resolution of comedy. The exposition over, the development may begin. Like all time references, Ania's question, "What time is it now?," marks the new section. The leitmotiv of sleep recurs, and bird song is heard again, this time on Chekhov's, not Stanislavsky's initiative. We return to a servant scene, the farcically accelerated seduction of Duniasha by Iasha. The next leitmotiv is the broken object: Duniasha drops a saucer (*The Cherry Orchard* smashes even more props than does *Three Sisters*). Duniasha's saucer is only the first symbol of a crashing world. Smashed crockery precedes the entry of the familiar Chekhovian dead, and the theme of the unmentionable past is expanded. The first ghost is the shadowy Ranevsky, Ania's father, who died six years ago; the second is a still more haunting phantom, her brother Grisha. Just like the first wife, Vera Petrovna, in *Uncle Vania* or the late Colonel Prozorov, father of the protagonists of *Three Sisters*, the ghost of a recently deceased person governs the behavior of characters in *The Cherry Orchard*—in this case the boy Grisha, who, perhaps by his tutor Trofimov's negligence, perhaps in the aftermath of his mother's bereavement, drowned in the river and provoked Ranevskaia's flight to France. Like *Macbeth, The Cherry Orchard* is besieged by ghosts: Varia is to mention two more, including Ranevskaia's nanny, and Lopakhin's brutal father also haunts the play.

The symmetry of this development is reinforced by Firs's entry, this time speaking words that make sense to the audience but nonsense to Varia, for in recalling the distant past he establishes the continuity of Paris as the real spiritual home of Ranevskaia's ancestors: "The master went to Paris once . . . by post-chaise." At this moment we realize the real pull on Ranevskaia's emotions is not now, onstage in the cherry orchard, but out of the play's time and space—six years ago and 1,500 miles to the west. Stanislavsky heightened this dramatic crisis with polyphony: while the revelations proceed, Duniasha and Firs prolong the preparation of coffee into a ritual for which Firs has changed livery, and Iasha shocks the gentry in the audience by smoking a cigarette. The rite of coffee-making over, Firs announces his impending death: "I can die happy" (literally, "I don't mind if I die").

As in the beginning of the act, Firs's scene heralds a mass entry, this time even more colorful: Ranevskaia has emerged from her coat in full Parisian dress and enters with Simeonov-Pishchik in semi-Asiatic clothes, the Ukrainian *sharovary*, and with Gaev miming billiards. The significance of the billiards (or, rather, snooker) terms may be random: Chekhov transcribed what the actor Vishnevsky heard in billiard halls. Billiards has a markedly ominous role in Russian literature—the first experience of life for the hero of Pushkin's *The Captain's Daughter*, the cause of suicide in Tolstoy's *A Scorer's Notes*. Here Gaev's obsession with the yellow ball may fit the play's chromatic symbolism (yellow is a fading, ugly color in Chekhov's spectrum). Gaev uses phantom billiards as a displacement activity, to hide embarrassment or distress, reenacting tricky shots to exorcise tricky social moments. Stanislavsky reduced the billiards feints to mere clowning: Gaev has a walking stick

Act 1

as a cue, as a means of touching. He is made to rest his stick on his sister's hand, and his hyperactivity was brought out in relief by a Pishchik constantly falling asleep, slumped against the furniture.

While Ania and Pishchik exemplify sleep, Ranevskaia with her coffee and Gaev with his imaginary cue embody wakefulness—the Macbeths that murder sleep. Lopakhin reintroduces the theme of time: twice he announces "time goes by" but meets with no response. Ranevskaia and Gaev show a different sensitivity: they do not listen, but their other senses perceive. "There's a smell of patchouli," Gaev complains disapprovingly—the first of many smells he detects. Smells usually emanate from Iasha, and patchouli was then, as now, considered a vulgar, overwhelming perfume. But note that Stanislavsky identified Ranevskaia as the source of the smell: in his notes for act 3 he asserted, "Ranevskaia has the Parisian habit of powdering herself and making sure she is looking her best frequently. She also abuses perfume, always having a bottle of it on her." On reentry she again speaks in exclamations, with extravagant body language, with a flurry of *liubliu* ("I love") that reveals her as the only sexual animal on stage.

Only by treating her as a female, rather than by pure reason, can Lopakhin attract her attention to the main theme of the play: the sword of Damocles, the auction threatening the cherry orchard, and the possibility of salvation. When Lopakhin mentions time passing, or a train to catch in two hours' time, Ranevskaia does not respond. But his calling her magnificent, declaring that he loves her "as his own flesh and blood" (*kak rodnuiu*), causes her to leap up and kiss the furniture. (Stanislavsky envisaged the coffee and the flattery rousing Ranevskaia to leap onto the divan, jump off, and rush around the room—to kiss her brother and weep as she embraces the bookcase.) She cannot absorb information: the announcement that nanny and the servant Anastasy have died leaves her unmoved. Brother and sister react only physically and instinctively: Gaev's second vice, his sucking of boiled sweets, appears. With one last desperate look at his watch—yet another appearance of time, the main protagonist of the play—Lopakhin broaches the real point: the cherry orchard can only be saved by destroying it, by chopping it down and leasing the land for development. Lopakhin's mathematics are the whole point of his argument, but he battles with a heroine so innumerate that she cannot even count the coins in her purse.

To the audience or reader Lopakhin is giving quite different information: his figure of 25,000 rubles a year at 25 rubles per *desiatina* (one hectare) reveals to the numerate how enormous, in fact hyperbolic, the cherry orchard is. This was the sticking point for detractors of Chekhov's plays: a cherry orchard of 1,000 hectares is unmanageable, it cannot exist in reality. To a less literal-minded and more receptive audience, the cherry orchard takes on from this point symbolic qualities: it represents an economic and social dinosaur approaching extinction. A cherry orchard that could glut the world with cherries and yet cannot earn its owners a living symbolizes a decrepit world, a decaying Russia for which ordered destruction is the only alternative to disordered ruination. Here, as Andrei Bely and Vsevolod Meierkhold perceived, the play leaves realism and enters symbolism: all Stanislavsky's attempts to heighten the reality could only increase the play's dreamlike quality. Lopakhin's figures and logic escape Gaev and Ranevskaia: they know that this orchard is unique. Ranevskaia points out that it is the only interesting feature in the province of Kharkov; Gaev—confusing fiction and fact in a bold stroke worthy of Borges—grounds the orchard in reality by telling the audience they will find it mentioned in their "Encyclopaedic Dictionary." Chekhov was one of Russia's most knowledgeable plantsmen: the dimensions of his fictional cherry orchard are no accident. With its notional 100,000 trees and 4 million pounds of cherries, it is meant to take on the mythical proportions of the Augean stables or the House of Usher. In his earlier settings, such as the labyrinthine house of 26 rooms in which *Uncle Vania* takes place, there is a hint of a mythical landscape, but *The Cherry Orchard* moves us on to a new spatial dimension.

One word in Lopakhin's argument disturbs the owners of the orchard—*vyrubit'* ("to cut down, to grub out")—and its crudity is so horrific that the subject is dropped. The comedy of deafness to reason develops: Firs distracts them with his bathetic, nostalgic anecdote of the past and extends the time scale of the play to "forty to fifty years ago," when the cherries were dried or marinated for the market to a forgotten recipe; Pishchik, prompted by mention of food, awakens and asks Ranevskaia whether she ate frogs. Here Lopakhin reveals a new mode—one that has puzzled interpreters—for the peasant and merchant gives way to the idealist, who claims to see in those that are going to lease the cherry orchard a new middle class. Throughout the act the past has dominated, but now the numbers evoke the future: "in twenty years" the country cottage owner will cultivate his hectare. Instead of prophesying ruin, Lopakhin foreshadows Trofimov and predicts a "happy and rich and luxuriant" orchard. It is tempting to see in Lopakhin the dream of capitalism and in Chekhov's political outlook a suspicion that there are as many illusions in capitalism as in the socialism of Trofimov or the feudalism of Firs and Gaev.

For the third time Varia's keys ring out doom. She unlocks the bookcase and hands a message from past time and distant space: the telegrams from Paris that will litter the stage. Ranevskaia's tearing them up tells us more about the lover she has fled than do her words "Paris is over and done with," or the other characters' abstention from comment. In Chekhov the tearing of paper is always portentous: Treplev's suicide in *The Seagull* is heralded by two minutes spent ripping up his writings. The telegrams that recur in acts 2 and 3 are climactic: Stanislavsky inserted two extra tense pauses—one before Ranevskaia accepts the telegrams and one before she tears them up.

One of the most famous comic set pieces in Russian drama ensues. Gaev, in yet another displacement activity to conceal his distress at his sister's louche love life, turns to the bookcase and delivers a centennial speech to it: "Most esteemed bookcase" has become a catchphrase in Russian (*Mnogouvazhaemy shkaf*). The effect of the speech, apart from the spectacle of everyone's embarrassment at this logorrhea (the third of Gaev's uncontrollable habits) is to characterize yet another male character as a dreamer at heart. Telling the bookcase that it "fosters within us ideals of goodness and social consciousness" links Gaev with Lopakhin and will link him with Trofimov. The Chekhovian male in this play, as in *Three Sisters*, is in thrall to the rhetoric of idealism. Here the idealistic rhetoric belongs to three time zones: Gaev's is that of the past, the 1880s of which he sees himself as the product; Lopakhin's is the rhetoric of the modern businessman who thinks he owns the present; Trofimov's is the rhetoric of the imaginary, anarchic future. In Chekhov's stories and earlier plays philosophizing is a form of mating display to attract the vulnerable Mashas and Irinas: here it is a displacement activity devoid of any communicative purpose. When Gaev realizes this, he reverts to his first vice, his involuntary phantom billiards.

Futile rhetoric leads the action into the secondary theme of thwarted love. After Pishchik's parody of courtly love, snatching from Iasha and swallowing Ranevskaia's supply of pills,[4] Lopakhin goes through mock-courtship of Charlotta, who is, compared with Ranevskaia, a mockery of the female "in a white dress, very thin, with a lorgnette hanging from her waist." Chekhov's manuscript has Charlotta consenting to perform ventriloquy and projecting a male voice offstage: "Who's knocking? It's my gentleman fiancé." (The published version of the play has Charlotta walking off, too tired for stage tricks.) Very slyly, Chekhov shows Lopakhin pointedly ignoring Varia as he takes his leave, and her telling him to hurry up and go away: his neglect and her anger signal frustration and jealousy. This presents our first interpretative problem: Chekhov's text does not provide the information an actor needs to decide why Lopakhin should torment Varia with animal noises and later quotations from *Hamlet* and, finally, a refusal to discuss marriage. Some producers have decided to make Varia physically so repulsive that all her sterling personal qualities count for nothing. Others, bearing in mind the asexual (or perhaps crypto-homosexual) nature of the male in this play, emphasize that Lopakhin, like Gaev and Trofimov, is "beyond" love, frightened by female expectations. A third explanation—which is plausible if we recall the explicit reflections of the narrator in the story that presages this play, "A Visit to Friends"—is Lopakhin's fears: marrying Varia would oblige him, as a virtual son-in-law, to indemnify the owners of the cherry orchard against their improvidence.

Before Lopakhin departs, he switches back to the main, financial theme: he again mentions a figure—a loan of 50,000 rubles. No sooner has he gone than the motif twists from drama into farce: Pishchik begs Ranevskaia to lend him 240 rubles for his interest payments. Pishchik represents the farcical counterpart of Ranevskaia's disastrous improvidence. Ranevskaia ends the coffee ceremony that has counter-pointed all the development, and we return to motifs of whiteness and cherry blossom that introduced the act. But the key is now altered: the sun gives light and warmth, and the bird song is friendly—starlings traditionally symbolize the spirits of the house. What the audience can see is projected offstage and into the past by Gaev and Ranevskaia reminiscing of things past: this time the imagery of sleep and awakening leads to passionate lyricism. The longing for the past, the exclamations beginning with "If only . . . ," are typical of Chekhov's middle-aged heroes and heroines, from Vania on, refusing to admit that their choices are irreversible. In *The Cherry Orchard* the unreal yearning becomes physical: Ranevskaia sees a young cherry tree as the ghost of her mother in white. It is a theme to be taken up in act 2 by Trofimov when he claims that the souls of the dead are in the leaves of the trees; it takes the action of the play out of naturalism and into a symbolist world. Stanislavsky reinforced the fantastic in what he called Ranevskaia's ecstasy of recaptured childhood by keeping up a counterpoint of noise: Firs mumbles, dogs bark, a gramophone offstage plays drunken peasants' cursing.

To put an end to ecstasy, a real ghost of the past enters: Trofimov reduces Ranevskaia to "embarrassment" (a stage instruction omitted in Frayn's version) and tears. Given the stereotypes in the minds of Russian audiences, the characterization of Trofimov caused Chekhov great difficulty. Chekhov compromises the voice of the future, the self-sacrificing idealist, by bringing out from the start a clash of Trofimov's noble ideas about freedom, vision, and renewal with his enslaved behavior, myopia, and worn tunic. The censorship helped Chekhov to degrade the stereotype: Chekhov was forbidden to explain why Trofimov is an "eternal student," to mention his being exiled and expelled from university for political activities. Typically, Ranevskaia's distress at the reminder of her drowned son switches to dismay at the sight of yet another physically inadequate male: Trofimov's hair has thinned and his sight weakened. Despite his youth, she treats him as preternaturally aged. Like Arkadina in *The Seagull*, no sooner has she rounded on one male than she turns on another, her brother, "You've aged, too, Leonid."

Two short farcical interludes herald the recapitulation of the main theme. First, Pishchik returns to the fray and gets his 240 rubles from Ranevskaia and Gaev; then we have the comedy of the insubordinate servant, as Iasha irritates Gaev with a new smell: "You smell of chicken." At his most absurd Gaev tends to be at his wisest, for he now sums up the dramatic predicament: that no imaginable means—inheriting wealth, marrying off a daughter, or begging from relatives—are feasible. The aphorism he uses is probably derived from one of Chekhov's professors of medicine. Chekhov, like Leskov, the novelist he so admired, liked to apply medical skepticism to life:[5] "If for some disease a great many different remedies are proposed, then it means that the disease is incurable." This kills off hope and gives the action a tragic note, reinforced by Varia's tears. Stanislavsky built up the solemnity by having Gaev slowly fill his pipe, recline on the divan, and wearily smoke, while Varia sits on a child's chair crying. But a glimpse of depths never lasts long in Chekhovian drama. From wise generality Gaev switches to foolish particularity, from general despair to the traditional comic reliance on a rich relative, the aunt in Iaroslavl, like the aunt in Penza on whom Chekhov's friend Aleksei Kiseliov so pathetically hoped.

Echoing Lopakhin's opening statements, Gaev switches his exposition back to Ranevskaia's past, adding touches that tell us as much about his snobbery as her loucheness: she married a commoner and is "depraved." This adjective has led many a director and actress to play Ranevskaia as a nymphomaniac, using her valet as a masseur onstage and a lover offstage, as though Gaev's puritanism were Chekhov's. Russia in the 1900s was more akin to Paris or Vienna than to London or Boston: the fact that a widow had a lover and that her family knew about it would not exclude her from society or destroy her self-esteem. Memoirs of foreigners in Russia (such as Gustave Lanson, tutor to Alexander III) confirm that the Russian gentry were the most broadminded in Europe; the behavior of Chekhov's sister, or of their women friends such as the writer Shchepkina-Kupernik, the actress Iavorskaia, or the schoolteacher Lika Mizinova, was far more libertine than Ranevskaia's. To see a condemnation of Ranevskaia's sexuality, rather than of Gaev's puritanism, is to misread text and mores. If

Act 1

Ranevskaia's character causes dismay in the spectator, it is a gradual process by which the audience judges her (like Arkadina in *The Seagull*) as an irresponsible mother and an unintentional embezzler. The dramatic function of Gaev's indiscreet condemnation is to abolish his momentary function as an objective commentator. Using the stereotype device of eavesdropping—Ania overhears this calumny against her mother—Chekhov puts Gaev back in his vice of logorrhea, a disease that takes him over as he promises to save the orchard and lays claim to being a man of conviction. The act takes place in the former nursery, after all, and it is easy for author and director to use this setting as a way of letting adult characters instantly revert to childlike behavior.

If act 1 thus completes its sonata structure with Gaev's recapitulation, we are now ready for the coda. The theme of sleep runs through all its tenses and moods in Russian: *spat', zasnula, usnula, spit* ("to sleep," "she has gone to sleep," "has fallen asleep," "is sleeping"). The motif of sleep—murdered, sought, or recovered—is a strong unconscious link between *The Cherry Orchard* and Shakespeare's *Macbeth*.

As Ania is led off to bed we hear an imperative, so reluctantly acted on by the characters. It concludes and unifies each act of the play: *Poidiom* ("Off we go" or "Let's go"). With Trofimov's final entry as a spectator, the act ends in music, the shepherd's panpipe, which reminds us we are in the south of Russia, where forest gives way to steppe and, for those who know Chekhov's imagery, reminds us of the death of nature in his 1887 story "Panpipes." Stanislavsky uses the story's imagery to build up a final impression of the South as the curtain falls. His instructions were, "The shepherd plays, you can hear horses snorting, cows mooing, sheep bleating and flocks of geese screeching. Birds are twittering. The sun rises and blinds the spectators."[6] No wonder Chekhov—perhaps more amused than irritated—told Stanislavsky, "One day I shall write a play that will begin, 'How wonderful, how quiet! You can't hear birds or dogs or cuckoos or an owl or a nightingale or a clock or bells and not a single cricket.'"[7]

6

Act 2

If we continue musical analogies and see act 1 as a typical first movement, carrying the main weight of the argument, organized in sonata
form, then act 2 is a typical second movement—slower, more episodic
and lyrical in structure. The frequency of Chekhov's direction *pause*,
which here occurs 16 times as opposed to seven in act 1 and not once
in act 3, proves the act's slowness. Given equal speed of performance,
act 2 is noticeably shorter than act 1 (acts 3 and 4 also decrease in
length of text). Act 2 divides into three sections: the first is an absurd
set of scenes in which servants parody their masters; the second is
dominated by Ranevskaia's passion and manipulation; and the last
brings Trofimov's diatribes to the fore. While act 1 was built around
the rising sun, act 2 reverses the process: the setting sun gives way to
the rising moon. Each act has its distinct lighting, appropriate for the
season: dawn, moonlight, candlelight, and daylight. But only act 1 has
accelerated time's velocity. Act 1 runs through two hours real time in
30 minutes stage time, whereas act 2, like acts 3 and 4, suspends the
conventional dramatic acceleration: the 20 minutes of the action may
represent little more in real time. In act 4 Lopakhin reminds us that
the 20 minutes left before departing for the station correspond exactly
to stage time.

Act 2

Stanislavsky treated act 2 as a slow movement: he weighed it down with more effects than the rest of the play put together and insisted on major alterations in Chekhov's text, particularly cutting a final scene between Firs and Charlotta as they search for Ranevskaia's purse and muse over horrors of the past. Disregarding Chekhov's distress at the zoological inaccuracies, Stanislavsky expanded the opening stage directions into a whole landscape, a mood picture, a pastoral symphony: "Last light of the sun. Summer. Haymaking. Heat. Steppe. The town is not yet visible in the mist. An insistent bird sings on one note. Wind sometimes runs through the foliage and makes a rustle. Far away the rye sways in waves (to be done with a lantern reflecting a beam in a sheet of tin). Occasionally a dry branch falls off. People are walking in the woods and you can hear broken branches crackling. A corncrake, frogs, songs, mist from a ravine." Chekhov's own instructions are less ambitious, designed to evoke melancholy: "an old, crooked and long neglected [*zabroshennaia*, Chekhov's most frequent adjective for gardens and other man-made landscapes] wayside shrine" with other memento mori, such as the old gravestones. The cherry orchard has now receded into the distance; the trees most prominent are poplars, whose associations in Russia are feminine pliability and the musky smell of new leaves in early summer.

In Chekhov's manuscript act 2 opened polyphonically: Ania in the background tells Trofimov about her unpromising efforts to get money from her paternal grandmother and the young couple are in flight from Varia's eyes. A few minutes later Varia is asking Charlotta to keep an eye on the couple and remember that supper is at nine. Both these episodes were cut, perhaps when Chekhov revised the text for the Znanie edition, where Varia's role as the zealous chaperone is only hinted at the very end of the act. In overhauling this act, Chekhov salvaged some of Charlotta's wistful speech from his final scene and used it to open the act. A biographical sketch upgrades Charlotta from a clownish caricature to a pathetic waif. But her props—a cucumber in her pocket and a rifle over her shoulder—are even more puzzling than her role in act 1. The cucumber, a Samuel Beckett type of prop, is part of the strange and untimely eating habits of the inhabitants of the cherry orchard; the rifle, however, to all who know Chekhov, is a prop that will be fired by the end of the play, if not, as Chekhov recommended in a letter to his elder brother Aleksandr, by the end of act 3. This play breaks with Chekhov's past not only in the absence of a love triangle and of a doctor: it has guns—Charlotta's rifle, Epikhodov's revolver—that never fire, a comic frustration of the spectators' expectations.

Just as familiar a Chekhovian prop as the rifle is Epikhodov's guitar: it links him to Telegin in *Uncle Vania*, another unlikely and tuneless guitarist of uncertain social status. Chekhov specified only the opening lines of Epikhodov's song—"What should I care for life's clamor, / What for my friend or my foe, / Had I a passion requited, / Warming my heart with its glow"—but they are the beginning of a "cruel romance" well known in the 1900s, and the audience, like Duniasha and the other listeners onstage, would suppose it to be the confession of a man convicted for the murder of the woman he loved. It contributes to the caricature of Epikhodov as a would-be murderous psychopath. Even to the nervous Duniasha Epikhodov's song is as empty a threat as the barrel of the revolver he produces. Like Lopakhin, Epikhodov is a parody of Hamlet, that honorary Russian citizen: his ruminations, inspired by his learned books, on whether to kill himself or to live correspond to Lopakhin's Hamlet-like rejection of the Ophelian Varia. In fact all the male characters of *The Cherry Orchard* talk in rhetoric like a literary parody. While Simeonov-Pishchik absurdly misapplies Nietzsche, or Lopakhin Shakespeare, Epikhodov surpasses them all: his complaint about life treating him "like a rowing-boat in a high sea" recalls the complaints of Gogol's Chichikov in *Dead Souls*; waking up to find a spider on his chest is pure parody of Dostoyevski (take Stavrogin in *The Devils*), as is his reading of the English historian Henry Buckle, a bête noire in the 1860s (for his disparagement of Russian barbarity). Epikhodov's pretensions are surpassed by Iasha's: when Iasha hears his masters approaching, he cruelly dismisses the infatuated Duniasha in favor of a cigar—a parody of the scene in Tolstoy's *Anna Karenina* when Koznyshev rejects the loving Varenka for a good cigar. Stanislavsky made sure that the farcical parody drowned out any sympathy this scene of doubly unrequited love might arouse: after all, the play's main action reduces the love interest to a minimum, and it is Epikhodov, Iasha, and Duniasha who provide the making of the traditional love triangle. By ensuring Epikhodov should trip over fallen branches as he leaves the stage and having Duniasha's kiss spoiled by cigar smoke up her nose, Stanislavsky's production kept farce dominant.

Just as the smell of patchouli or chicken linked a servant episode to a master's episode, so the opening of the second section of act 2, when Ranevskaia, Gaev, and Lopakhin take over the stage, is signaled by a smell: "Who's smoking some foul cigar?," asks Ranevskaia. The new scene is constructed in the same way as the first: intersecting monologues that in the distance or on the page would appear to be dialogue. Just as Charlotta, Epikhodov, and Duniasha in turn bewail their sensitive natures and unhappy fate while going through the outward motions of a conversation, so Lopakhin, Gaev, and Ranevskaia, apparently immersed in conversation, barely interact at all. Lopakhin weaves the strongest thread, taking up the theme of act 1, the imminent sale and the need for a decision. As the irritation grows into fury, his sentences become shorter and shorter, and when the inanity of the responses he gets is intolerable, his statements and questions turn into abuse. But even when he shouts "old woman" at Gaev, there is no direct reaction. Ranevskaia's mind is on a different track, pursuing vulgarity, guided by her nose. After Iasha's cigar she recalls the smell of soap on the tablecloths of the restaurant where they have just had lunch. She reacts to Lopakhin's proposal in the same way, as if it were just another bad smell: "summer cottages—summer people—forgive me, but it's so sordid." Gaev just breathes physical satisfaction: a lunch to digest, a game of billiards to play, or physical irritation. Iasha, aping the gentleman, is Gaev's own horrible image in a distorting mirror.

But irrelevance is only a surface feature of Gaev's and Ranevskaia's speech. The social and political theme that is to rise in Trofimov's diatribes in the third and final section of act 2 is broached when Ranevskaia looks in her purse (before spilling its contents) and remarks that the kitchen is feeding the estate's hangers-on nothing but pulses, while she is "mindlessly spending." Her extravagance surrounded by destitute peasants gives sustenance to Trofimov's rhetorical protest. Gaev's reported conversation with the waiters at lunch, on the 1870s and on decadents, brings back the theme of anachronism: Gaev pledges allegiance to any time—to the 1870s, the 1880s—but the present and misses his ironic affinity to the decadents. What, after all, is the final sentence of the ultimate decadent play, Villiers de l'Isle-Adam's *Axel*? "Living—our servants will do that for us."[1] By that criterion no character in Chekhov's work is more of a card-carrying decadent than Gaev, still utterly in the tutelage of Firs: his functioning as a male is delegated to the antics of the unspeakable Iasha.

Lopakhin's furious outburst and threat to walk out does not bring the owners of the orchard to their senses, but it darkens their mood: the theme of "the millstone on my breast and shoulders ["neck" in Frayn's version] . . . my past" that was provoked by the telegrams from Paris in act 1 now reemerges as the theme of sin and retribution. Ranevskaia feels the house about "to come down about our ears," the word *sin* echoes through her outburst, the longest uninterrupted speech in the play.[2] As Ranevskaia's speech nears its climax, she shows that this fit of passion, too, is provoked by a telegram from Paris: she pulls it from her pocket and rips it up. The shadow of the offstage arbiter, the lover in Paris, grows larger, and the audience is fed a little more information on the missing years. Ranevskaia now has a fuller biographical sketch than any other character. She has Furies—two dead, one alive—in her wake: apart from a drowned son, her late husband, a commoner, a spendthrift and an alcoholic, and a sick obsessive lover hounding, robbing, and betraying her. We begin to understand why she should refuse to concentrate on the sale of the estate: her return is not that of the prodigal, but, rather, she has been rescued by her dependants from suicidal despair. Comedy threatens to become melodrama, and would do so were it not for that sudden childlike switch, so typical of her, from passion to hypersensitive sense impression. Just as she detected the smell of cigars, so she and Gaev suddenly hear what the ordinarily perceptive Lopakhin cannot hear—the distant music of the Jewish orchestra. The frivolous idea of act 3, hiring the Jewish orchestra to play at a party, is suddenly born as if the misery of a minute before were entirely obliterated.

This irruption and subsidence of past passion was greatly reinforced in Stanislavsky's production. He had Lopakhin put his hat on the ground, force himself onto the bench next to Ranevskaia and Gaev and, with increasing violence, strike his knees, rub his foot, stand, pace the ground, raise his voice, and revert to the peasant. When he shouts at Gaev, Lopakhin is made to spit, get on his knees, tear his hair, beat his breast, and elbow Gaev away when the latter seeks to detain him. Ranevskaia's reluctance to discuss the auction was developed by Stanislavsky into a reluctance to be in Russia: "She loves strolling," Stanislavsky noted, "along the Boulevard des Italiens in Paris, but not on Russian country roads. Her dress is seasonal, but Parisian. She has a handbag with a handkerchief, a French novel and a purse, perfume and smelling-salts."[3] The theme of escape abroad was emphasized by having trains pass in the distance and a telegraph messenger pass on a bicycle, with Ranevskaia waving desperately at him for her telegram from Paris. The more Lopakhin insists, the more Ranevskaia evades him: she leaps onto a sheaf of hay and chews the stalks. Her speech on her sins was to be played lying down.

Stanislavsky had Gaev evading Lopakhin's truths by protracting his phantom billiards, teasing Ranevskaia, and fishing for her dropped handbag with his stick. He, too, lies down while his sister confesses, but Stanislavsky's major innovation to motivate their inattention was mosquitoes. From their entry to their departure they slap at biting mosquitoes. "NB. Don't forget the mosquitoes," Stanislavsky recorded twice more, in the middle of Ranevskaia's and Trofimov's major speeches.[4] The mosquitoes were the most important of Stanislavsky's additions to survive: in his notes the instructions to arrange for a chorus of peasant women to cross backstage on their way back from haymaking were canceled—no doubt after Chekhov's irritated protest at the excess. But 10 minutes' swarming of imaginary mosquitoes is ample proof: Stanislavsky heeded Chekhov's wish not to drown the vaudeville in melodrama.

Once Ranevskaia has spoken, she recovers her dominant position and can counter-attack. Lopakhin is on the defensive and after praising a provincial comedy now has to call himself, not Gaev, a "stupid oaf." Ranevskaia's attack on the grayness of the men around her seems quite uncalled for (it recalls the counter-attack of Elena in *Uncle Vania*): "What gray lives you ["they" in the Frayn version] all live. How much you say that should never be said at all." This is a part of her female frustration, which is to come out in the same way when she counter-attacks Trofimov in the following act. The sequence here also antici-pates act 3, for no sooner has she achieved dominance of the males on stage than she starts match-making: Lopakhin is pressed into marrying Varia. Then, as though to prove Ranevskaia's point about Lopakhin's and Gaev's inadequacies, Firs enters, bringing Gaev his coat. Gaev, pursued by his clothes, is as tied by Firs to his wardrobe as he was by his rhetoric to his bookcase.

Servants in Chekhov herald the immanent themes. After Firs, Trofimov approaches with Ania and Varia and major political polemics in tow. But it is Firs who introduces the political note. What his uni-form said in act 1 is now articulated. Firs has not accepted the Emancipation of 1861: he views it as catastrophe, not liberation. However antiquated and reactionary his views may seem (to Chekhov's or to today's audience), however much Lopakhin may mock him with "Lovely it was before. At least they flogged you," Firs's nostalgia and skepticism are wise in their senility. His phrases—"And I remember, everyone was glad. But what they were glad about they didn't know themselves. . . . The peasants belonged to the masters and the masters to the peasants. Now it's all chippety-choppety—you can't make any sense of it"—echo the authorial voice in Chekhov's stories of the 1890s, such as "Peasants" or "In the Gully." In the great Volga famine of 1890–92, with the peasantry abandoned to the clutches of debt and tax collectors, epidemic disease and crime led many thinkers—liberal or socialist—to agree with Firs that the emancipation had worsened, not improved, the peasantry's condition. *The Cherry Orchard* takes on a political dimension: it nudges the audience into viewing the bankrupt orchard as a model of a country ruined by progress.

Heralded by Firs, Trofimov's arguments with Lopakhin and even with Gaev at first resemble the traditional mating display of Chekhovian males before an audience of eligible females—a pattern Chekhov inherited from Turgenev's novels, in which the idealist defeats the sophist and wins the love of the naive girl. But the pattern was deconstructed by Chekhov: idealist and sophist ignore each other,

Act 2

the debate is two simultaneous monologues, and neither girl nor orator are aware of competition or reward. Moreover, Chekhov has widened the comic disparity of reality and mask by presenting Trofimov— prematurely aged, personally unadventurous—preaching a cult of youth and ruthless decisiveness.[5] The very appearance of Trofimov to the peasant mockery of Lopakhin—with a bouquet of flowers gathered by Ania, a pile of books, and an oak walking stick— belies his rhetoric.

At this point Stanislavsky stressed the solidarity that makes women the ruling oligarchy in *The Cherry Orchard.* When Ania and Varia appear, they all leap onto the haystack into Ranevskaia's embraces: "They don't kiss, they lick each other. They grunt and squawk for lack of air, and laugh when their kisses hit a ticklish place, like an ear. . . . Ranevskaia fights back with hay and finally they throw it all over her, almost burying her." While Trofimov talks, Ranevskaia quietly sings and moves in time to the Jewish orchestra playing French music hall songs in the distance.

The strictures of Russian censorship inhibited Chekhov from giving Trofimov an overt political program to preach. But the signals his words give off are clear to the audience. Trofimov begins as a materialist, telling Lopakhin that predatory capitalists are necessary for "nature's metabolism"; then Varia asks him to talk about the planets. When Ranevskaia suggests he take up yesterday's topic, "The Proud Man" ("Pride" in Frayn's version), the spectators know what Trofimov respects—Maksim Gorky's most Bolshevik play, *The Lower Depths,* in which the inhabitants of a doss house are roused from submission by a revolutionary who preaches an ideal "proud man." Trofimov's first speech is neither a parody nor a rallying call. It is a fair summary of a typical Russian student's ideological vade mecum: the cult of work, which Chekhov's characters often preach, but seldom embody. "Trofimov smokes as he paces, counting his steps and looking at the ground. That's how students say clever things,"[6] Stanislavsky notes for his production, showing once again that he saw the main characters all "playing a comedy" in their poses and images of themselves.

As in act 1, Gaev surprises the audience with a sudden aphoristic piece of wisdom: "It makes no difference—you still die" (five syllables in the Russian: *vsio ravno—umriosh'*). This is the shortest but the most authorial and authoritative of the contributions to the only debate onstage in *The Cherry Orchard*. (After this curt put down, Stanislavsky's Gaev replaces his lorgnette and returns to his newspaper.) Trofimov's response seems to veer from materialism to idealism and to deny death: his speculation that perhaps we have 95 senses that survive the death of our five blends with the extrasensory perception of atmosphere and the future that Gaev and Ranevskaia keep revealing.

Trofimov's third and last speech to the company, however, comes back to reality. It repeats phrases from Chekhov's letters and reiterates the speeches of the heroic doctor Khrushchov in *The Wood Demon* and the flawed doctor Astrov in *Uncle Vania*, denouncing the idle words of Russia's intellectuals who preach and pontificate while their servants live in filth and reforms exist only on paper. The difference between this speech and that of Chekhov's doctors is that Trofimov does nothing that backs up words: he reconciles no enemies, he plants no trees. But Trofimov's words "I have little love for all those serious faces; I fear those serious conversations. Better to be silent" echo Chekhov's letter of 1896 to Nemirovich-Danchenko: "We so rarely have serious conversations. When people are silent, it means they have nothing to talk about. . . . We have no politics, we have no social or salon life, not even street life, our urban existence is poor, monotonous, wearisome, boring" (No. 1825). Trofimov's "Most members of the intelligentsia, so far as I know it, are seeking nothing, neither the truth nor anything else. They're doing nothing. . . . They all philosophize away" parrots phrases from Chekhov's letter of 1899 from Yalta to Ivan Orlov, a country doctor he had known in Melikhovo: "The whole intelligentsia is at fault, all of them, sir. I don't believe in our intelligentsia, hypocritical, idle. I don't even believe when it is suffering and complaining, for its oppressors come from its own loins" (No. 2655).

Trofimov's indictment was too strong for the censor: the lines "And right in front of their eyes the whole time there are workers living on filthy food and sleeping without pillows to their heads, thirty and forty to a room—and everywhere bugs, damp, stench, and moral squalor" had to be replaced. What Chekhov patched this cut with

Act 2

seems just as strong and even more in accord with similar passages in his letters and elsewhere in his plays. The lost patch reads, "The overwhelming majority of us, ninety-nine percent, live like savages, at the slightest provocation brawling, swearing; they eat revolting food, they sleep in filth, in stale air." Yet the censor decided to let this pass.

For a moment Trofimov has become an authorial raisonneur, but the moment a very brief one. Lopakhin takes over the role, as the only man who claims to know life in the real world outside. At this point Trofimov and Lopakhin seem not just allies but positive figures. No wonder naive radical spectators of the play saw them as a band of brothers retrieving a hopeful message from the ruins of *The Cherry Orchard*.

Between the end of Trofimov's speech and Gaev's announcement of sunset, Stanislavsky originally planned a mute mime: "A mosquito scene. The air is quiet, only a bird is calling. The mosquitoes are overpowering, a new swarm has arrived. Slaps on cheeks, foreheads, hands are constantly heard. Everyone is sitting pensive, killing mosquitoes. Gaev is reading a newspaper. Finally, at the end of the pause, he rolls it up, rustles it and puts it away. He takes off his monocle."[7] Chekhov replaced this dumb show for the revised version of the act, making Ranevskaia dismiss the message of hope and Epikhodov kill it dead as he passes backstage playing his guitar. In this interpolation[8] individual speech seems to lapse: phrases pass from character to character as if in a meaningless poem. The interchange "There goes Epikhodov. . . . There goes Epikhodov. The sun has set, ladies and gentlemen. Yes" has a primitive rhyme and an eerie assonance of *d* and *t* in the Russian: *Epikhodov idiot. . . . Epikhodov idiot. . . . Solntse selo, gospoda. Da.* The phrase suddenly brings to life the apparent etymology of the name Epikhodov, "walking about," which makes him a comic Satan, walking to and fro over the earth. The act is now shifting key. Inspired by this dreamy mood and the sunset, Gaev begins a prose-poem in praise of nature, a pastiche of Turgenev at his most saccharine (Stanislavsky has him compose it sprawled full-length on the hay). Then, when Gaev is forced into silence, we hear the famous "noise of the breaking string" that has made this play so famous: "Suddenly there is a distant sound, as if from the sky: the sound of a breaking string—dying away, sad."

73

This sound is associated with Chekhov's early work, with stories of the south of Russia, with the steppe undermined by mineshafts and hidden cables, even with the setting of his juvenile *Platonov* (sometimes known as *Fatherlessness*). Gaev and Trofimov lose all credibility, attributing the noise to a bird, a heron, or an eagle owl. Lopakhin shows his solidarity with the author by correctly identifying the noise: "Somewhere a long way off, in the mines, a winding cable has parted." The noise of the breaking string is associated in Chekhov's work with the death of nature, industrialization, the crippling of human beings; this threat from an underground world to the frivolous gentry on the surface conveys some of the numinous horror of the Morlochs in H. G. Wells's *The Time Machine*. Stanislavsky knew very well the crucial importance of this sound, which is also to end the play, and gives precise instructions for achieving it: "Stretch from the beams to the floor three wires (probably the sound will depend on the metal the wire is made from), one thick wire (and the density of the sound will depend on the thickness), a second thinner wire, and a third still thinner (perhaps made of different metals). Pass a thick piece of rope over these wires. The first sound denotes the mine-bucket falling. The others are the echo, i.e., the sound wandering over the steppe. To accompany or finish this scale of sounds, a light tremolo on the big drum (thunder)."[9]

Lopakhin gives the explanation familiar to the author, if to few of the spectators; Firs steps in with an interpretation that is ignored by the characters but must have had a far deeper effect on the audience. Like Gaev and Trofimov, Firs, too, associates the breaking-string noise with a bird, but this time with the bird of ill omen, the tawny owl, and the folk belief that howling samovars or stoves betoken catastrophe.[10] Yet again we recall *Macbeth*: Lady Macbeth hearing "the owl scream and the crickets cry." But by disaster ("troubles" in the Frayn version) that the breaking string has foretold in the past Firs means not regicide but the Emancipation of 1861. This raises the political level on which the play operates from interpretation to prophecy, for the catastrophic Russo-Japanese war and the 1905 revolt that followed Chekhov's death were events as cataclysmic for Russia's social structure as the emancipation 40 years before.

Act 2

Fixing this momentary insight into the future, a drunken passer-by intrudes, the first of several intruders in *The Cherry Orchard* who suggest the newly insolent and insubordinate lower classes. A polite inquiry and tubercular cough are a pretext for declaiming civic poetry of protest, if not revolution—a line from Semion Nadson's poem "My Friend, My Brother, Weary, Suffering, Sad"[11] of the 1880s and one from Nikolai Nekrasov's poem "Go to the Volga. Hear Again the Song It Sings" of the 1850s. Chekhov used Nekrasov in his stories to signal the peasants' and workers' sacrifice of blood, sweat, and tears for the comfort of the upper classes. The passerby is menacing not just because he is a drunken aggressor but because he underlines the hint of literally subversive forces beneath the cherry orchard. Stanislavsky suggests, "Let the audience suspect something ominous in this figure or let them understand that it is unpleasant to meet such a gentleman at night in the woods."[12] To get rid of the threat, Ranevskaia squanders money for the second time in this act and the third time in the play. The scene ends with the older members of the cast hurrying off and, after a brief, grotesque parody of Hamlet and Ophelia by Lopakhin[13] and Varia, a date two months hence (22 August) suddenly looms for the auction (and for act 3). Time has crystalized for the spectator, if not for Ranevskaia and Gaev: Stanislavsky has them singing in carefree harmony with distant peasants as they vanish into the setting sun.

Trofimov and Ania are left alone for what Stanislavsky decided would conclude act 2. They talk of not the desperate near future but the hopeful distant future, with Trofimov's "bright star" guiding free and happy mankind. Trofimov reinterprets the orchard to Ania, whom he has taught not to love it. He shifts the boundaries of space as boldly as he does the confines of time. He also broadens the allegorical scope of the play by proclaiming "All Russia is our orchard." This is not just a repudiation of private property. It is a declaration, perhaps unconscious, of national bankruptcy; it turns the play into an elegy for a dying class and a dying system. As we shall see, it is not the first time that Chekhov uses a doomed orchard to symbolize his country's political system on the verge of extinction, but it is the first time that his drama has reached out into the preserve of the Russian symbolists, eschatology, and historiosophy—the study of the end of the world and of the meaning of history. Like Firs, Trofimov sees the cherry orchard as a monument to serfdom; like Ranevskaia (with whom he has passion and rhetoric in common—though his passion and rhetoric are intellectual and hers sensual), he sees ghosts in the cherry trees. In act 1 Ranevskaia sees her mother in the blossom; in act 2 Trofimov sees the serfs' faces in leaves and tree trunks. Trofimov's first tirade to Ania ends with a typically Chekhovian conceit of 200 years between now and the Kingdom of Heaven—a faith Chekhov had mocked in his journalism and through half-cynics such as Astrov in *Uncle Vania*.

This speech was too strong an indictment of Russia's landowners for the censor. An entire sentence was cut: "Owning living souls—it's changed something deep in all of you . . . at the expense of people you don't allow past the front door." Chekhov's patch for the cut is now omitted and his original words restored, but, toning down the denunciation, Chekhov in fact devised a poetic flight of fancy for Trofimov, heightening the motif of passing centuries and his feeling for the trees as living beings: "Oh it is horrible, your orchard frightens me, and when you come through the orchard in the evening or at night, the old bark on the trees reflects the light dimly and the cherry trees seem to be dreaming of what happened a hundred or two hundred years ago, and they suffer from bad [*tiazhiolye*] dreams."

The sole escape from bad dreams in Chekhov's work is flight: just as Chebutykin in the last act of *Three Sisters* advises Andrei to "keep walking, without so much as a backward glance," so Trofimov's parting advice to Ania is to "throw the keys down the well, and go." But Trofimov is incapable of irony: he ends with a passion that, once again, oddly recalls Ranevskaia. Like Chebutykin, they both advocate flight from nightmare situations "without so much as a backward glance" (*bez ogliadki*). Both use the phrasing of Christian penitence: Ranevskaia has spoken of her sins, begging the Lord for mercy; Trofimov likewise ends with "we have to redeem our past . . . and it can be redeemed only by suffering." The half-affectionate, half-antagonistic relationship between Ranevskaia and Trofimov is mirrored in the idiolect they share, their capacity for confessional exaltation. Trofimov's second speech to Ania (which Chekhov inserted after Stanislavsky cut the final moonlit scene of Charlotta and Firs) also recalls Ranevskaia's speech: it, too, is a confession of privation and suffering. Ranevskaia is no more a "landowner" than Trofimov is a "student": they are acting, and overacting, a part.

Gaev had stifled rhetoric by announcing that the sun had set; his niece Ania (although she seems enthralled by Trofimov) downs this new flight of words by announcing that the moon is rising. In the final version of the play the act ends on an upbeat note, with Trofimov's ecstatic (and unjustifiable) premonition of happiness. The slower, quieter ending Chekhov had envisaged, which would have added several minutes to the act, introduces Firs's confused memories of a murder and Charlotta's morbid reflections that Chekhov salvaged for the opening of the act. As they search for the money Ranevskaia dropped (Stanislavsky noted, "Epikhodov has trodden on whatever Ranevskaia has lost") Firs and Charlotta murmur about death and the *salto mortale* and, as she takes a bite of her cucumber, Charlotta reminds Firs that it is time he was dead; the action closes with Firs's meaningless "twitch, twitch," which is a far more gloomy coda than the major key of the revised version. (This coda anticipates the final scene of act 4.) To this gloom, before Stanislavsky decided to cut it, were added devilish effects reminiscent of *The Seagull* or Chekhov's story "An Incident in Practice." Charlotta sets fire to a piece of wood and fills her mouth with flames: "A train passes and you can see a red lamp moving against the backdrop. Mist condenses. A chorus of frogs cries louder. A corncrake and distant dogs barking." Only the last effect, as the curtain falls, with Varia officiously calling Ania to supper, was preserved in both versions.

It is hard to see why Chekhov assented to Stanislavsky's opinion that dramatic tension was lost in the original version: it is in this cut that the conflict between author and director is sharpest. In his memoirs Stanislavsky apparently relented: "After such an animated scene between the young people, such a lyrical ending depressed the mood of the act, and we couldn't raise it again. Obviously, this was our fault and the author had to pay for our inability."[14] But there is one powerful argument for accepting Stanislavsky's cut: as act 2 ends we hear the same imperative "Let's go" or "Come on" as Ania is led away, this time by Trofimov.

7

Act 3

If we persist with Meierkhold's perception of *The Cherry Orchard* as a symphony, then the third act is fast—it has not a single *pause*—and is a classical scherzo, with a minuet and trio structure. Here in fact the analogy is most convincing, for act 3 is dominated by the rhythms of the quaintly old-fashioned dance music played by the Jewish orchestra that was heard in the distance in act 2. The *grande ronde*, the quadrilles, and the *lezginka* (in 6/8 time) that they dance all support the mood of a scherzo, while the serious interpolations, such as the row between Ranevskaia and Trofimov and the catastrophic finale, play the same contrastive role with the dancing and other games as the recurrent trio theme plays in the classically binary minuet or scherzo form. While Chekhov gave music a greater role in each successive play (compare with act 4 of *Three Sisters*), only the third act of this play, with its almost continuous orchestral accompaniment, can be classified as musical drama.

Act 3 is one of the most difficult 20 to 30 minutes to stage in the theater: its set requires a large drawing room, separated by an arch, or even a floor down, from the hall, with a glimpse into, or at least the sounds from, the billiards room. It even has, in Stanislavsky's concep-

Act 3

tion, a sight of a conservatory, as well as a hint of stairs down to the sets of acts 1 and 4. The action has to be choreographed so that the dancing couples reach the front of the stage in time for their dialogue; Pishchik's organizing of the dance, Charlotta's magic tricks, and the station master's recital are in effect theater within the theater. Together with the Jewish orchestra just offstage (visible in many productions), the onstage action requires extraordinary ingenuity to coordinate.

While Stanislavsky made no changes to the text, he felt constrained to rearrange Chekhov's ball and expand the party. His initial interpretation seems inspired. He describes the mood this way:

> A complete failure of a ball. Not many people. Despite all efforts, they couldn't find more people. It was all they could do to get the station master and post master. A soldier (the son of a civil servant) in coarse soldier's clothing (uniform), a shop assistant wearing a jacket and red tie, a young boy (son of the old woman), dancing with the tall thin priest's daughter, even Duniasha has been recruited. Half the dancers don't know the steps of the quadrille, let alone the *grande ronde*. . . . The audience looking at those dancing is even sparser. They are sitting around in the doorway, backs to the spectators. You can see the priest's wife, and old officer and his wife, an old woman in black. Iasha is leaning on the doorframe looking at the dancers. . . . In the billiard room Epikhodov and the neighbour's manager, a benevolent old German with an imperial beard and a pipe, are playing a game. The noise of billiard balls goes on almost all evening. Silence reigns all evening. You'd think everyone was there for a requiem mass. When the dances stop they all freeze on chairs along the wall. They sit and fan themselves. The moment anyone shows a sign of animation—running past or talking loudly—everyone is embarrassed, and the guilty person, ashamed of the disorder he has provoked, becomes even more embarrassed and silent. . . . The food on the table is sparse. . . . Fresh nuts, apples, soda water. The soda water has been drunk and there are no new bottles. When the dancing is over, the Jewish musicians smoke in the hall, as do the smokers among the guests.[1]

Stanislavsky has caught the desperation of Ranevskaia's ball, the most inauspicious act 3 party since Macbeth's banquet, and, like that banquet, it is ruined by ghosts and bad omens.

Stanislavsky opens act 3 with several minutes of dancing. He also crowded the stage with twice as many characters, for apart from those mentioned by Chekhov and already added in Stanislavsky's "mood" evocation, he adds a school teacher, a schoolboy, and schoolgirl in Ukrainian dress; the telegraph messenger and teacher's wife; the local policeman and no fewer than three more priest's daughters. At the end of Stanislavsky's notes for act 3, still more characters were added: among them Pishchik's daughter Dashenka (whom Chekhov meant to keep unseen, the source of Pishchik's outlandish opinions), a hair-dresser, a fat landowner and his thin wife in silk crinolines, the miller, the midwife, a Jew ("decent, intellectual . . . Semitic melancholy"), his wife with her tasteless diamonds, his pale-faced son in a dinner jacket and his daughter-in-law ("who sniffs spirits and abuses her migraine pencil"). On reflection, Stanislavsky removed the Jewish family from the cast but decided to make the policeman a music lover who plays folk songs on the flute. If Chekhov's ball had begun with too few guests, Stanislavsky turned the evening into a gathering of the entire district.

The merits of Stanislavsky's elaborate opening are that Pishchik's total exhaustion when Chekhov's dialogue starts is perfectly plausible. As in act 1, Pishchik is caricatured as a creature reduced to needs for food, sleep, and money—a reductio ad absurdum of Ranevskaia and Gaev. Announcing desperate indebtedness and mislaying his wallet in the first few minutes of the act makes him still more a parody of Ranevskaia. To this caricature Chekhov adds new touches: the audience can tremble lest he fall down dead, when he announces "Blood pressure—that's my trouble, I've had two strokes already." They can also associate him with Epikhodov as a misinterpreter of ideas, when he reports his daughter's assertion that Nietzsche authorizes forgery. The spectacle of the sweaty old man intermittently biting an apple, falling asleep, and quoting Nietzsche while a ball and billiards go on around him takes this act out of the bounds of realism into a surreal world. It heralds symbolist drama, such as the opening scene of Aleksandr Blok's *Neznakomka* (The Strange Woman) of 1908,[2] where characters dance in an inn, discussing various cheeses. The whole concept of a party swamped with unknown faces on the very day when the fate of the doomed estate is to be decided has the catastrophic horror of symbolist drama; the entire texture of the act is nightmarishly surreal in its mixture of trivia and horror, laughter and anguish. Stanislavsky developed several of Chekhov's latent ideas: the nuts that in act 1 Charlotta alleged her dog ate play a prominent part in act 3: not only are they served, but Iasha steals them and Ranevskaia (in a touch that Stanislavsky later thought better of) even throws one in Trofimov's face.

The dancing briefly gives way to eating and to a fit of anxiety that overcomes Pishchik, then Varia, then Ranevskaia; the scherzo mood resumes with Charlotta's sequence of card tricks, ventriloquy, and conjuring Ania and Varia out of thin air. Stanislavsky makes the conjuring, like the dancing, a mass scene, with an audience onstage crowded around Charlotta, bewildered by all sorts of other effects— metallic noises she makes when she taps Pishchik on the skull, a pack of cards retrieved from the policeman's neck, ventriloquial noises coming from the bellies of the priest's daughters. The diversion has its omens: the cards guessed at represent the gap between fate and aspiration. Trofimov guesses the queen of spades (the harbinger of destruction in Russian literature ever since Pushkin's story of that name), while Pishchik, loyal admirer of his hostess, chooses her ideal, the ace of hearts. The greatest irony is that Charlotta the clown shows such sleight of hand, whereas Epikhodov, Duniasha, Ranevskaia, Lopakhin, and Trofimov all break things or collapse. These mass scenes emphasize the solitary tension afflicting Ranevskaia. In rehearsals, Stanislavsky told one French director, he had forced Olga Knipper to express the maximum tension: Knipper "takes cup of tea from Firs, drops cup, which breaks."[3] To ensure that Knipper dropped the cup, "Stanislavsky told the stage manager to put boiling water in the cup. And he did." Stanislavsky wanted "all animation to fall away" and the guests to slink back from the drawing room into the hall. The switch to a minor key is heralded by yet another breakage, Iasha announcing that Epikhodov has broken a billiard cue. The verb "to break" is as important to this play as it is to *Macbeth*.

The scene that follows is the longest continuous buildup to a climax in the whole play, the only moment at which Chekhov is Ibsenian, for here there is a real confrontational dialogue and real antagonism between two forces—a libertine woman and a puritanical boy. Ranevskaia appeals in her misery for male comfort, even for salvation: her key word is her Christian name, *liubov'* (love), but for Trofimov "love" is linked with his key word, *poshlost'* (vulgarity). The more she presses Trofimov, the more he retreats. From calling her *dorogaia* ("my dear") he takes refuge in formulas like "I sympathize with all my heart." With each speech Ranevskaia moves from comedy to melodrama. Stanislavsky notes that "she throws herself on Petia as if in a French melodrama." At the same time, Ranevskaia moves from fecklessness toward wisdom, as she reproaches Trofimov for his intolerance and inexperience. Here the character grows so rounded that Olga Knipper was justified when in the 1920s she told the English critic Hugh Walpole "that Mme R. was not wholly feckless, that her speech about her return to her lover in Paris showed this, and that the cherry orchard was sacrificed for many reasons."[4]

In contrast to the dogmatic, blinkered student, Ranevskaia momentarily achieves tragic grandeur by appealing (against all the evidence) to her roots and to the memory of the dead, from her grandfather to her son. Her words recall those of the heroine of "A Visit to Friends": "I was born here, my father and mother lived here, my grandfather. I love this house. Without the cherry orchard I can't make sense of my life." Then the bubble is pricked: she reverts to her matchmaking self and offers Ania in marriage to Trofimov. Her Parisian self overcomes her Russian image, as Trofimov picks yet another telegram from Paris off the floor. (Stanislavsky has him hand it to her as a gesture of contempt.) Powdering her face and putting on perfume like warpaint, Ranevskaia then resumes her habitual vindictive domination of males who have failed her. She teases Trofimov about his hairless face and his virginity. Her frank avowal of passion for an unworthy

Act 3

lover is devoid of irony: the imagery is laden with fateful associations. When she talks of her love, saying yet again *liubliu, liubliu,* she adds, "He's a millstone round my neck—he'll take me to the bottom with him." And, by evoking drowning, she brings up the death of her son Grisha. While there is more than a hint of Lady Macbeth unmanning her collocutor, this interchange—like many confrontations in Chekhov's plays between a mature, passionate woman and a callow, dispassionate youth—echoes act 3 of Shakespeare's *Hamlet,* where the sinful Gertrude defends herself against the reproaches of Hamlet, her puritanical son. Although Chekhov's episode is recognizable as a dramatic row in which the antagonists use all the ammunition available, it ends as a thoroughgoing farce: the shocked Trofimov runs off and falls downstairs. The sudden switches in Ranevskaia's tone from passionate and tragic to manipulative, abusive, farcical, and reconciliatory show, however, that the passion is not to be taken seriously. Ranevskaia (though only an amateur) is an actress, playing a part with such hamming melodrama that she must be considered the heroine of her own private comedy.

Meierkhold's interpretation of Ranevskaia's role here is persuasive:

The leitmotiv of the act is Ranevskaia sensing the gathering storm. Everyone around is living dimly: look at the self-satisfied people dancing to the monotonous jangling of the Jewish orchestra and, as in a nightmarish whirlwind, whirling in boring modern dances. . . . [T]hey don't know that the earth on which they are dancing, is slipping from under their feet. Only Ranevskaia senses Catastrophe, expects it and rushes about, and for a moment stops the moving wheel, this nightmarish dance of marionettes in their puppet-theater. And with a groan, she dictates crimes to people, to stop them being prigs, because through crime one may arrive at sanctity, but through mediocrity nowhere and never. The act acquires the following harmony: Ranevskaia's groans with her premonition of imminent Catastrophe (the element of fate in the new mystic drama of Chekhov) on the one hand, and the puppet-theater of marionettes on the other hand.[5]

Farce brings back the guests, and the scherzo resumes. Now it is dominated by the station master and his recital of A. K. Tolstoy's "The Scarlet Woman." This poem was extremely well-known to Chekhov's contemporaries, and he had mentioned it in three of his early stories (in one it comes as a ludicrously inappropriate recital piece at a civil servant's jubilee). Here, just after Ranevskaia's failure to win over Trofimov, "The Scarlet Woman" is the most tactless choice the station master could have made, for the poem is about Mary Magdalene boasting of her seductive powers and then meeting John the Baptist, who subdues her with a glance. After this earlier fragments of the play seem to whirl past in the dance: Firs and Iasha clash, Pishchik begs for money, Epikhodov, with his usual mention of invertebrates, pleads with Duniasha. But in the middle of this disintegration of the play's motifs the conventional tragic messenger appears. Ania reports that an old man has called in at the kitchen and said that the estate is sold. Unlike conventional drama, the message is vague, and Iasha refuses to go and confirm it: the dancing and Charlotta's transmogrifications— she appears in drag—carry on. Here Stanislavsky wanted the music at its loudest and the dancing at its wildest.

Chekhov's mature plays always adhere to one classical convention: disaster happens offstage, and the audience is forced to wait for an announcement. We see this in the seduction in *The Seagull*, the duel in *Three Sisters*, and the auction in *The Cherry Orchard*. Sometimes the curtain falls before this announcement, as at the end of *The Seagull*; sometimes the dramatic suspense is exploited in the conventional way. Chekhov makes the wait almost unendurable by introducing yet more comic turns. First Firs reintroduces the motif of the wrong garment— Gaev is wearing his lightweight coat—then Iasha begs Ranevskaia to take him with her to France. After shocking us with his tactless joy at the prospect of losing the cherry orchard, Iasha takes the audience back to one of the staples of European comedy: the barbaric, rabid Francophile who—to quote the Danish dramatist Ludvig Holberg (*Jean de France*) or the Russian Denis Fonvizin (*Brigadir*)—has his body in Denmark or Russia but his soul in Paris. When offstage catastrophe finally supplants farce in this act it amounts to the suspended reentry of the minor theme. Varia accidentally strikes Lopakhin with a billiard cue, and catastrophe arises. The suspense is unbearable: there are no verbal messages. The first signals are olfactory: "You smell of brandy, my dear fellow," Pishchik tells Lopakhin, while Gaev, wiping away tears, just hands Firs a packet of anchovies and salted herrings. Here the audience will remember it has been a long, hot summer's day and will imagine the smell. In Chekhov's work, smelly fish was always a distraction from uncomfortable truths. One famous occurrence in the story "The Lady with the Lap Dog" is the remark "The sturgeon was off" from the hero's friend, who has refused to listen to the former's confession of love. Lopakhin's silence and Gaev's tears give no confirmation of the result of the auction. At the sound of the billiard balls Gaev stops crying and goes off to change for a game. "I advise the actor [playing Lopakhin]," wrote Stanislavsky, "to forget for the time being about any joy, on the contrary to express embarrassment and awkwardness as much as possible."[6] But once again the drama switches to the melodramatic mode, and Lopakhin's drunken speech, announcing his betrayal of his friends and his triumphant loyalty to his class, gathers pace. He roars with laughter, stamps his feet, and jangles the keys that Varia has thrown onto the floor.

The first impact of the speech is the characters' feeling that the worst has happened. But the delayed information is perhaps the reason that Ranevskaia is to recover her composure so quickly, by the start of act 4. Lopakhin announces that for the estate he has paid 90,000 rubles (nearly $500,000) over the debt, enough money—not forgetting 15,000 rubles from the aunt in Iaroslavl—to allow Ranevskaia to return to France and support her lover for a few more years. The tragedy is in the humiliating turning of the tables, a peripeteia that Chekhov and other dramatists have used before and that the Chekhov family had itself experienced: the businessman who was to help them in insolvency has profited by it. The owners of the cherry orchard have been betrayed, if not beggared.

The jangling of the keys that Varia has abandoned is a prompt: the Jewish orchestra tunes up, and Lopakhin's aggressive orders to them and his promise to take an ax to the trees and create new life has horrible political implications, as if a pogrom were about to begin. Despite momentary condolence, Lopakhin leaves the scene like a parody of a Russian merchant on the rampage, smashing tables and candelabras,[7] declaring, "I can pay for it all." Lopakhin's exit tells us that he is just as fatal for vulnerable objects as Ranevskaia and her servants. It is worth remembering that Stanislavsky (born Alekseev) came from the merchant classes and understood the extravagant, violent ecstasy behind Lopakhin's vandalism. "To justify Lopakhin what he must have is 'an artist's enthusiasm,'" Stanislavsky urged. The orchestra strikes up again, and Stanislavsky has Lopakhin dance "a vulgar polka," to tie in with the dances that opened the act.

In conventional productions all movement now stops: in the drawing room downstairs act 3 ends, just as act 4 of *Uncle Vania* ends: a middle-aged victim sits crumpled up, weeping inconsolably, all illusions lost, while a young girl on her knees improvises new illusions, a fairy-tale consolation full of images of paradise and promises of new life and joy. Stanislavsky wanted the stamping and shouting of the dancers, as they speed up from the polka to the wild *komarinskaia*, to be heard from the hall, behind closed doors, while the sound of billiard balls grows louder. Ranevskaia's weeping was to be punctuated by the sound of plaster falling off the ceiling. But the main echo in our ears as Ranevskaia cries is that final word to each act in the play, *Poidiom* ("Let's go" or "Come"), this time spoken not to Ania, but by her.

8

Act 4

Producers find Chekhov's fourth acts difficult to stage, especially those of *The Cherry Orchard* and *Uncle Vania*, which are aftermaths to the grand climaxes of the third acts. When the stage is littered with baggage, and little is happening but embarrassed departures, there can be no dramatic fireworks: these last acts are not only more subdued but shorter than the other acts. It has even been suggested that some of Chekhov's fourth acts are interchangeable. Certainly, our analogy with classical symphonic structure weakens here, for act 4 is no classical finale (even though its slow tempo and dark ending make a comparison with Tchaikovsky viable). But anticlimax does not make act 4 a failure: Chekhov's purpose in his dramas and many of his stories is to show, as in the art of gardening, that the end of a structure is only the beginning with our understanding deepened. Act 4 mirrors act 1: it takes place in the nursery again, characters once again worry about time and trains and talk of Paris, this time in the future, not the past.

Originally, however, act 3 was to be set in the desolate, half-cleared, half-wrecked set of act 3's party: Stanislavsky envisaged an apocalyptic opening, with the chandelier's wires dangling from the ceiling, nails sticking out of the wall, patches of bright paint where pictures once hung, furniture and baggage stacked along the walls. In the final version, set in the nursery, desolation is more subtly suggested, and the luggage stacked backstage. What Stanislavsky envisaged as funereal wailing Chekhov changed to just peasants saying farewell.

The bottle of champagne that Lopakhin brings to see the old owners off is an ironic piece of continuity: it reminds us of the coffee in act I, the station buffet in act 2, and the brandy in act 3—drink to stave off the inexorable. Again Iasha acts the traditional comic insubordinate by drinking the champagne, just as he broke the billiard cue and (in Stanislavsky's additions) stole the nuts. This time, however, Iasha is not sneering but rejoicing at the prospect of returning to France. Gaev and Ranevskaia, Chekhov emphasizes, are untouched by the traumas of the past months: the theme of squandering and the purse, which this time Ranevskaia gives away, show improvidence as a permanent attribute.

Once the continuity has been established, the countdown starts. Lopakhin gives the season—October—and the time left—20 minutes—which in most productions is no more and no less than real time in the theater. Lopakhin's character then shows a new side: his dialogue with Trofimov is the only prolonged affectionate interchange between two characters in the whole of Chekhov's work. Though their outlook on life is different, they share a common disdain for the estate, a common willingness to see the orchard cut down. Above all, neither has sufficient interest in the opposite sex to provoke rivalry. Their dialogue begins with teasing banter and soon moves to intimacy. Trofimov uses the formal *vy* address to everyone else in the play, but with Lopakhin he briefly ventures an intimate *ty*, first of all in anger in act 2. In act 4 he takes his cue from Lopakhin, and most of their interchange is in the *ty* form.[1] Trofimov's teasing—telling Lopakhin not to wave his arms about—warms to affection: "All the same, I love you ["I can't help liking you" in the Frayn version]. You've got fine sensitive fingers, like an artist's. You've got a fine, sensitive soul, too." Here culminates the recurrent motif of hands—hands that shake, are kissed, drop things, are gloved or ungloved, and wave about, which is the key expressive mode in *The Cherry Orchard*.

Act 4

The play's eligible bachelors address their affection not to Varia or Ania but to each other: there is an intriguing resemblance to Aleksandr Blok's symbolist drama *Balaganchik* (*The Puppet Theater Man*), where in the last act Pierrot and Harlequin make up their differences and ignore Colombine. It is, at the very least, a cogent reason that Varia should be so bad-tempered, interrupting the tête-à-tête, hurling galoshes across the stage. Lopakhin's offer of money and Trofimov's refusal to accept it show a generosity of spirit and a common cult of independence that raises them (and Charlotta, who sometimes wears men's clothes) above the rest of the Gaev household. Lopakhin and Trofimov now establish male solidarity, reminding us of act 2 of *Three Sisters* and the banter between Tuzenbakh and Vershinin. Lopakhin asks, "Will you get there?," and Trofimov concedes that it might be posterity, not himself, that will reach the promised land. His confidence in mankind's march to truth and its eventual reward—"[I'll] either get there, or else show others the way"—echoes Vershinin's faith in work and the new happy life. He tells Tuzenbakh, "then at least my descendants, and their descendants after them."

This mood of optimism and hope is cruelly punctured by the noise of axes striking the cherry trees. The noise of metal on wood is used threateningly by Chekhov in stories and plays—usually the night-watchman marking the hours through the night on a rail in the garden—but never with such menace as here. The second omen of death is Ania, Iasha, Varia, and Epikhodov discussing whether Firs has been sent off to the hospice. This is the only reference to the doctor (who has never received the letter about Firs), a character most puzzlingly absent from the play. Iasha's callousness now takes on grotesque proportions. He is more than a *Jean de France*: he is a monster, and his failure to take care of Firs is compounded by his unfeeling refusal to say good-bye to his mother (as in act 1 he refused to greet her) and by a psychopathological indifference to Duniasha's tears. Some productions show Duniasha in act 4 heavily pregnant, though one might think fertility as unlikely as any other sign of vitality in *The Cherry Orchard*.

As always, the entry of Gaev hard on Iasha's heels is marked by his olfactory sensitivity. Nothing he sees or hears is as noticeable as what he smells: "Who is it smelling of herrings?" The comedy is not just that the impeccably spruce Iasha smells of chicken, cigars, or herring; it is in the heightened sensitivity of Gaev and Ranevskaia to the insignificant. Half-time in the act is marked by Ranevskaia announcing that there are only 10 minutes to go (few plays give an audience as much notice as *The Cherry Orchard* of when to pick up their belongings). Lopakhin and Trofimov's reasoned optimism now gives way to a quite irrational optimism among the gentry. Without a tear Ranevskaia parts from the house she declared she was inseparable from: the audience might then recall that the cherry orchard is, after the villa in Menton, the second house she has lost. Ania, her "eyes sparkling like two diamonds," expresses pleasure and, misled by a tubercular misfit, looks forward to a new life in town. Gaev's optimism is even more incredible: financially the most incompetent hero even in Chekhovian drama, he confirms that he has a job in a bank, thus reiterating what the audience originally believed was sheer fantasy. In act 2, when he announces the bank's offer, Ranevskaia dismisses it—"The idea! You just stay as you are"—just as she dismisses his remark that a general in town "might put up something against my note of hand" with the explanation, "He's living in a dream. There's no general." In act 4 the impossible has apparently come true: unlike conventional comedy, vice is triumphant and improvidence rewarded, for Ranevskaia has the 105,000 rubles and Gaev a salary of 6,000 rubles a year. The young are to walk off unendowed and unmatched, while the old incarnation of sin is now cushioned with money, returning to her partner. The values of Molière's comedies have been turned upside down.

The world of act 4 is as lenient as it is unjust. Firs is abandoned to die, the faithful Charlotta is homeless, and Varia is expected to keep house for strangers. Yet Ranevskaia declares that she is sleeping better—yet another odd echo in her characterization of Lady Macbeth. The improvident but serendipitous Pishchik has become rich: porcelain clay has been found on his land. The ludicrous Epikhodov—one of the most incompetent servants to be found even in Chekhov's work—is the one household employee to be retained by Lopakhin, which raises doubts about Lopakhin's business acumen or his profitable fields of poppies. Chekhov implies the misrule and unreason of the cherry orchard has infected the world outside it. The countdown goes on: Ranevskaia announces they have five minutes left. The scene in which she uses these five minutes to exercise her match-making talents for the last time is enough, in fact, to demolish Lopakhin as a hero. To the giggling of Ania and Charlotta, and the empty bottle of champagne, Lopakhin and Varia are shut in the nursery for the expected betrothal. (Those who have read Chekhov's stories know that all such encounters end in a nonproposal and a discussion of the weather.) This nonproposal is one of Chekhov's finest comic scenes: Lopakhin, looking at his watch before he even begins, announces that he has given special protection to Varia's worst enemy, Epikhodov. Male and female then discuss the different directions they propose to leave in, and finally Lopakhin takes refuge in the neutral topic of the weather. The same frost that opened act 1 ("three degrees of frost") chills act 4 with overtones of the porter in *Macbeth*: "This place is too cold for hell." In Chekhov's plays we emerge where we came in, but we are worse off, for, as Varia remarks, "our thermometer's broken."

That last remark, before Varia collapses sobbing and Lopakhin rushes to answer a probably prearranged call, operates on many levels. It is yet another ominously broken object, like the saucer, the billiard cue, and the hatbox Epikhodov has squashed—part of the disintegration of the estate. It also symbolizes the loss of all capacity for objective measurement. Even to a pre-Freudian psychologist of sex it proves Lopakhin's sheer lack of libido. Directors and actors have hesitated in motivating Lopakhin. Can such a dynamic male really refuse such an ideal and loving wife as Varia would appear to make? Is his initial fixation on Ranevskaia the explanation for why he first besieges this woman with advice and then betrays her and for why he does not look at any other woman? Or is Varia just physically repulsive? In an analogous situation, however, in *Uncle Vania*, where Dr. Astrov refuses to propose to Sonia, Sonia's ugliness is explicit. Lopakhin's indifference, even fear, is in perfect harmony with Trofimov's "We are above love" and Gaev's contentment sucking sweets and playing billiards. Chekhov admired the Austrian writer Leopold Sacher-Masoch, after whom masochism was named and whose plays and stories portray increasingly libidinous females and increasingly jaded males. *The Cherry Orchard* takes this contrast to absurd extremes.

Twenty, ten, five, and finally zero minutes is announced by Trofimov. In the final parting only the embraces of brother and sister express pain. The play pretends to be over, but this is Chekhov's greatest ending. None of his plays manages to achieve such unexpected and powerful finality—a scene comparable with the silent tableau of horror that ends Gogol's play *The Government Inspector*. The stage is empty for as long as a minute; the only sounds are doors locking and axes striking trees. But there is one character we have seen in all the previous acts whom we have not yet seen in act 4. Firs first entered the play staggering across a deserted stage, and he does so again. Firs, whom the most cynical audience would assume that even the irresponsible Gaev and Ranevskaia would take care of, shuffles in, makes a short speech and lies down to die. His last mumbling words take the play into a new sphere—more Samuel Beckett than Chekhov—and suggest that not only the orchard but the entire world is unreal: "My life's gone by, and it's just as if I'd never lived at all." The words stop at the point of the inexpressible, and we hear act 2's musical note of the breaking string take over—this time to be superseded by the distant noise of axes.

In the ending of act 4 we can sense how apt was Meierkhold's comparison of the play to a Tchaikovsky symphony, for its last minutes are like a Tchaikovsky coda, in which any of many bars could serve as the last. There are several points, once the characters leave the stage for good, at which the curtain could fall,[2] and each point would determine retrospectively the mood of the whole play. The audience has already been conditioned by the previous three acts to expect the curtain to fall on *Poidiom* or *idiom*, the latter of which is uttered twice after Gaev's last billiard mime—this time evoking the white ball (omitted in the Frayn version)—by Ranevskaia and then by Lopakhin. But the curtain does not fall. Ania and Trofimov then utter a "Farewell, old life" and "Hail, new life." Still the curtain stays raised: this optimistic note is not to be the last chord. A last ghost is evoked: as in act 1, Ranevskaia recalls her mother. Lopakhin's brusque last words, ending, "Good-bye then" (in Russian a businesslike, smug slang *Do svi-*

dantsia), also fail to bring down the curtain. The pathos takes over as Gaev (*in despair*) and Ranevskaia (full of apostrophic "Oh"s) call farewell: still the curtain does not fall on our pity for them. In Trofimov's call of "Hulloooo" from outside, the mournful Russian vowels *au* (which locate someone lost in a forest) provide the next possible ending. Then Ranevskaia's "We're coming" (*idiom*) signals to the audience that the play is really over: spectators reach for their belongings as silence reclaims the stage. Like the unexpected last bars of a Tchaikovsky coda, Firs appears. Firs, as in every other act, worries about Gaev's clothes, but the motif of devotion has lost its endearing comedy and taken on a horrific implication: the irrelevance of all preoccupations in this desolate setting and final hour. Of all Chekhov's strokes, this shows the most prescience: in bringing on the old man to mumble inanities and die, it is as though Chekhov had seen in a vision Samuel Beckett's *Endgame* or even the horrors of history that feed Beckett's drama. As Chekhov had predicted in 1892, in a letter to Aleksei Suvorin, "Anyone who invents new endings for a play will open a new era" (No. 1184).

How Stanislavsky interpreted the last few minutes of the play, we do not know, for his notes peter out on Lopakhin's last exit. Theatrical tradition disagrees as to whether Firs is doomed to die or not. If he dies, the old and new owners of the cherry orchard are murderers. Some directors and critics insist that this is implausible, that Firs is just resting and will be found by Epikhodov. The evidence is against them, however, for the theme of Firs's death is steadily built up. Frequently lapsing into senile mumbling, he has stayed alive only in order to greet Ranevskaia. Iasha, Epikhodov, and Charlotta (the latter in the scene excised from act 2) all tell him it is time he died. Certainly all those associated with the first production of the play assumed that Firs's final appearance heralds his death. Stanislavsky's notes for the previous three acts all imply a struggling Firs on the verge of losing all his faculties. The ghastly tableau quality and the autumn stillness of this final scene in the slanting light of a fading October afternoon are nonsensical unless they signal the entry of death into the play. *The Cherry Orchard* would be a very odd play indeed if it lacked not just a love triangle, a doctor, and a gunshot but death as well.

Even the most hardened spectators, as they leave the theater, having seen the last movements of Firs and heard the noise of the axes on wood, would not feel they had been present at a comedy. Where is the triumph of youth? Where is betrothal overcoming all obstacles? Where is the return to normality and the exposure of abnormality? The spectator will recall the play's comic moments—caricatures and incarnations of comic vices; stock farcical actions, from eating a cucumber to falling downstairs; comic devices such as irrelevant responses in dialogue, rapid volte-face in subject, attitude, and tone. And the spectator will realize that he has been misled by the initial stock comic situation: two unmatched couples, two older people whose vices block a marriage, the desperate need for a financial windfall, servants who exceed their duty. He will realize that, because he has been misled by traditional expectations that are thwarted, this is a comedy in which the joke is against the audience—an anticomedy. Each of the main characters is in fact comic in the most literal sense: they are playing a comedy, in the French and Russian sense of the phrase, putting on an act. Ranevskaia's and Gaev's rapid mood changes, their switches from flippancy to emotion, are the changes of comic actors going through their repertoire. Trofimov, too, is acting the part of the radical student—and Lopakhin that of the peasant turned merchant—to the point of parody.

Chekhov has thus redefined the word *comedy*, but his subtitle "comedy", however much we are compelled to accept it, still puzzles us. All the ingredients are there and the tempo gathers speed, but the final scattering and destruction belongs in our minds to tragic drama. The text of *The Cherry Orchard* does not itself provide a basis for understanding the play—even when we look at it in tandem with what we know of Stanislavsky's authentic, contemporary staging; even when we extract information and opinion from Chekhov's letters, reported remarks, and notes, as well as those of his contemporaries and successors. Chekhov's work is an integrated whole, and to deepen our understanding of the play we have to look at it in relation to what preceded it—first in Chekhov's writing and then in his reading. In other words, we must look at the intertextuality of *The Cherry Orchard*.

9

The Metatext: Some Verbal and Nonverbal Elements

Reading *The Cherry Orchard* reminds us how important in Chekhov's drama are elements other than speech: not just auditory but visual and even olfactory signals to the audience. The silences and inarticulate gestures and the sets and the props are more than adjuncts to the text: Chekhov integrated them into the drama as no playwright before him had done.

Some nonverbal elements are licenses to director and actor to improvise gesture and mood: the typically Chekhovian instruction *pause* is one. It also functions as a tempo marking. Note how acts 1 and 4 have a moderate number (7 and 11) of pauses, but the slow act 2 has 16 and the fast, music-driven act 3 has none. If we add the pauses to other moments of silence—preceding the breaking string, or the empty stage before Firs appears in the first and last acts—then a production of *The Cherry Orchard* can pass a fifth of the time without a word spoken. Add to this the musical element, which sometimes counterpoints speech and sometimes takes over from it, and clearly the play is more than the sum of its utterances.

The music of the Jewish orchestra is first heard faintly in act 2 and comes to the fore in act 3. Its archaic tunes suggest the anachronism of the Ranevskaia-Gaev household and the lost zeitgeist to which they are loyal, but once the orchestra controls the movement of the characters it reduces them to puppets, takes hold of their speech rhythms (Ranevskaia hums the *lezginka* at one point), and gives the audience a message about the characters' lack of control or free will. Such musical messages are intelligible, but others (less so in *The Cherry Orchard* than in earlier plays) were meaningful only to Russian audiences of the day; they have been lost to audiences of other times and nationalities. Chekhov gives characters snatches of song—from operetta or the music hall—that ironically comment on the action. Nobody has yet traced Lopakhin's snatch of song in act 2—"Money talks, so here's poor Russkies Getting Frenchified by Germans." Its significance is lost to us. But Epikhodov's ill-sung opening words from a "cruel romance" do give us a key to his culture.

It is Iasha's two lines of song from act 3, however—"And will you know just how my heart beats faster?" (*Poimiosh' li ty dushi moei volnenie?*)—that have the strongest allusive power. Chekhov assigns this song to the arrogant and heartless servant, Borkin, in the first (1887) version of *Ivanov*, and there, too, it signaled the singer's callousness. It was a woman's song (composed by N. S. Rzhevskaia) and one of the most popular romances in Russia in the 1880s. Literally translated, it goes, "Will you understand my soul's emotion, the sad grief of fateful thoughts and the shy fear of involuntary doubt and what draws me into the mysterious distance? Will you understand? (*four times*). Will you understand whom I call for, whom I entreat to understand me fully, how I languish, how much I suffer, how ardently and passionately I love? Will you understand? (*four times*)." On Iasha's lips the song mocks Duniasha's infatuation and echoes Ranevskaia's passionate speech of a few minutes before: Iasha is not just parodying but parroting his mistress. The song operates here just as it did 17 years before in Borkin's mouth, where it makes fun of Ivanov's deplorable search for new happiness and desertion of his loving wife. The servants' vaudeville culture deeply subverts their masters' romantic aspirations. But vaudeville culture lacks permanence: today nobody acting Iasha can rely on his audience knowing Rzhevskaia's song to make Iasha's heartlessness obvious.

The Metatext: Some Verbal and Nonverbal Elements

The cherry trees that burst into the set of act 1 and that die so obtrusively and audibly in act 4 are the dominant nonverbal communicators. In act 2 Stanislavsky, as we saw, supplemented these dendroids by adding both Chekhov's poplars and the noise of broken branches as characters made their way on or off stage. The trees are more than visual and auditory signs. As in *Uncle Vania*, here characters lean through the windows backstage to reach out to them. In act 1 first Varia and then Gaev and finally Ranevskaia turn their backs on characters and audience to communicate through the window with the trees. We are confronted with Chekhov's strange dendrological symbolism: throughout his work (stories and plays) the trees that ordinarily figure as symbols in the great Indo-European myths play a lesser part. Rarely does he refer to oaks, never to ash trees or to beeches, whereas the slender, vulnerable trees of the Russian north—poplar, birch, and willow—or trees that symbolize the vulnerable human, such as the maple with its palmlike leaves, recur in Chekhov's settings. The fruit trees that die of neglect symbolize human mismanagement of nature from his earliest to his final work. If we take the hyperbolic orchard and garden of Chekhov's only novel, *A Shooting Party* (1884), we find exotic bergamots and other neglected trees conveying the same mournful message as the plum tree in the story "The Bride" (1903) or the cherry trees of this last play.

Trees in Chekhov have a Celtic mythological value: they are repositories for human souls. Trofimov tells Ania in act 2 that there are human faces and voices in every tree trunk, leaf, and cherry. Trees are the only living creatures who evoke a response from alienated human beings. Elsewhere in Chekhov's work the abandoned orchard mirrors the decay of its human caretakers. Families in decline are approached along an avenue of rotting lime trees or decaying firs (e.g., "The House with the Mezzanine" of 1896), thus the orchard's demise must herald its owners' doom. Chekhov's trees often share the values attributed to them in Russian folk song: the poplar as female beauty, the maple as human warmth, the cherry blossom as erotic fervor. Folk symbolism stems from a culture common to audience and playwright.

Trees make an impact that is more than visual: they rustle in the wind and groan under the ax. But most underrated in Chekhov's work is the importance of scent. The slight bitter almond smell of cherry blossom in act 1 should dominate the theater, masking the patchouli or "boiled chicken" smells that offend Gaev. In act 2 the musky scent of the new leaves of the Russian poplar should likewise suggest over-powering sensuality that nobody but Ranevskaia can exude and that should override the smell of Iasha's cheap cigars. Once disaster strikes, the trees recede and the scents onstage are comically gruesome: act 3's final atmosphere is contaminated by Gaev's herring and anchovies, which linger on into act 4 (Gaev complains that Iasha smells of her-ring). Smell is used by Chekhov for both serious and farcical effects. While the trees are mean to pervade the stage with a sensual power the characters lack, the pungent smell of stale fish is a distraction from emotional reality, a talisman against family quarrels and amatory dra-matics, a pin prick in the dramatic balloon.

The Seagull has an explicit passage, where Trigorin—the only writer-hero in Chekhov's mature work—tells Nina how he loathes fashionable sickly smells, such as heliotrope and mignonette. Chekhov put his own distastes into Trigorin: he endows Gaev not just with his medical lore but with his fastidious sensitivity to vulgar smells. The patchouli that Ranevskaia (or possibly Iasha) scents act 1 with was the most vulgar perfume Chekhov could have chosen. He may have read the chapter on perfumes in Joris-Karl Huysmans's notorious novel Against Nature (1883–84), where the Faustian decadent hero (appro-priately named Des Esseintes), searching to alleviate his boredom, deserts words and pictures to compose in perfumes: "in the end he resorted to Patchouli, the bitterest of the vegetable aromas, which sug-gests both mould and rust."

To see in Chekhov's last play the beginning of a theater of smell would seem far-fetched were it not for a coincidence in time: the fan-tastical German poet Christian Morgenstern, shortly after The Cherry Orchard, was writing his "nonsense" poems about Korf and Palmström, who, like Des Esseintes, experiment with composition in perfume: "Palmström builds himself a smell-organ and plays Korf's Wild Garlic sonata on it. This begins with triplets in alpine herbs and gives joy with its acacia aria. But suddenly and unexpectedly in the scherzo, between tuberosa and eucalypt, follow the three famous wild

The Metatext: Some Verbal and Nonverbal Elements

garlic places."[1] Chekhov may be said to have achieved what Morgenstern only fantasized about in his *Theater I*: "Palmström works this out for himself: a square theatre with a stage. . . . [Y]ou smell, with the authentic smell of earth, grasses and flowers blossoming on their own roots."[2]

Morgenstern's idea of a new theater of scent and vegetation is perhaps no coincidence: he was passionately interested in Russian literature, translated much "new" drama (Ibsen and Strindberg), and had been enthralled by the performances of the Moscow Arts Theater when it visited Berlin in 1906.

10

Intertextuality: Chekhov's Texts and *The Cherry Orchard*

The word *Chekhovian* suggests that the writer's works have noticeable unity of structure, style, and mood. *The Cherry Orchard*, too, derives its essential elements from both plays and stories. To take the dramatic structure first, we find that the play—opening in spring and closing in autumn—roughly follows the time structure of *The Wood Demon* (and its later revision as *Uncle Vania*), *The Seagull*, and *Three Sisters* (where the spring of act 1 and the autumn of act 4 are two years apart). This is a pattern Chekhov followed for 15 years. (His earlier plays, *Ivanov* and *Platonov*, both open in early summer but have no marked progression of seasons.) The location of Chekhov's plays is likewise a constant: except for *Three Sisters*, set in a semi-Arctic town, the plays take place in a rural retreat. Generally, Chekhov's plays are located on the west-to-east "fault line" between north and south, between forest and steppe, where Russians interact with Ukrainians and with Jews. (*Uncle Vania* in fact is set, like *The Cherry Orchard*, with Kharkov as the nearest town.)

In all Chekhov's plays from *The Wood Demon* on, visitors from the metropolis (St. Petersburg, Moscow, Paris) arrive, destroy the peace of the permanent residents, and then leave, themselves intact. This consistency of time progression and location determines a consistent plot: hope yields to disillusionment, as budding leaves become falling leaves; the mobile and urbane tyrannize the immobile and provincial. (This consistency of plot is breached only by *The Wood Demon*, where the happy conciliations of act 4 are quite unlike the typically Chekhovian end of *Uncle Vania*.) Just as the shortening days of autumn signal time expiring, so the fixed location is itself under threat. The bankruptcy of *The Cherry Orchard* perpetuates the bankruptcy of *Platonov*, the proposed sale of the estate in *Uncle Vania*, the paralysis and penury of Sorin's farm in *The Seagull*, and the three sisters' relentless eviction from their house.

As well as the division between migrants and residents, the cast in Chekhov's mature plays tends to be grouped by several criteria into conflicting parties: old versus young, masters versus servants, activists fighting the system versus quietists accepting the system, and, above all, male versus female. In *The Cherry Orchard* the groupings are particularly complex, so that each character opposes other characters in a variety of ways. Trofimov can be contrasted with Gaev as "youth," with Ranevskaia as "male" and as "resident," and with Lopakhin as "activist." *The Cherry Orchard* stands apart, for no love triangle among the gentry cuts across or motivates these divisions and no doctor arbitrates them. But the play's oppositions develop those of early plays: when Trofimov and Lopakhin argue on the keys to mankind's happiness, they take up positions—revolutionary versus evolutionary—similar to those adopted by Tuzenbakh and Vershinin in *Three Sisters* and by Astrov and Vania in *Uncle Vania*— even to those of Treplev and Trigorin in *The Seagull*, where literature and the theater stand for general ideas and real life. The much more conventional comic "anti-servant," with his hyperactive insubordination, goes back to the Mephistophelean saboteur Borkin in *Ivanov* and is developed through the estate manager Shamraev, who holds the household of *The Seagull* hostage with his refusal of horses and his grossly insulting flattery, into the clowning devilry of Epikhodov. Iasha, too, can be traced back to Borkin: both smoke cigars too lordly for their rank.

The main identifiable difference between Chekhov's later plays and the earlier work is the dominance of females. Although the opposition of an inactive and active female is to be found in *Ivanov* between the dying Sarra and Ivanov's new love, Sasha, it is only in *The Wood Demon*, *Uncle Vania*, and *The Seagull* that the division between the girl in black—despairing but aware of the world—and the girl in white—optimistic and naive—develops, reaching a clear opposition in *Three Sisters* (Masha and Irina) and *The Cherry Orchard* (Varia and Ania). As we shall see, the color symbolism in the heroine's choice of black or white is Chekhov's tribute to Maupassant, but he fits it to his own tendency to cast women as predators or prey—Varia rushing out like a spider to deal with the servants' misdemeanors or Ania innocently enthralled by Trofimov's and Ranevskaia's promises of happiness.

The center of Chekhov's late comedy is, however, the irresponsible mother—a figure owing something to Shakespeare's Gertrude (*Hamlet*) but more to Turgenev's and Balzac's dramatic heroines. The woman who refuses to face up to her responsibility as a mother or a stepmother is the nearest to a fairy-tale villain in Chekhov's work. Beginning with Elena in *Uncle Vania*, she becomes a Chekhovian archetype in Arkadina (*The Seagull*) and Ranevskaia. Their perversity with money (Arkadina is avaricious and Ranevskaia a spendthrift, but neither provides for anyone but themselves), their closeness to a brother whom they desert, their freedom from marital ties, and, above all, their desertion of their offspring—whether the writer Treplev or the schoolgirl Ania—make Arkadina and Ranevskaia of the same stock. We can find the key to Chekhov's idea of comedy and of woman as an actress by comparing *The Seagull* to *The Cherry Orchard* and their heroines to each other—women who constantly play a role and who defy the realities of age. Arkadina is a professional and Ranevskaia an amateur, but both are innate actresses.

The dominance of woman in Chekhov's later plays has much to do with the effeminacy of the bachelor male. Gaev resembles Sorin in *The Seagull* as much as their sisters resemble each other. Both long for amusement, both are bullied by their roving sister and by their servants, and both have become buffoons. They are dismissed by male outsiders (Dr. Dorn and Lopakhin, respectively) as "old women." Like

Uncle Vania Gaev no sooner begins a monologue than his niece tells him to shut up. Just as the older males form a chain of characters, a chain also links the younger male protagonists in names beginning with "T"—Treplev in *The Seagull*, Tuzenbakh in *Three Sisters*, and Trofimov in *The Cherry Orchard*. All are attached to a girl in white (Nina, Irina, or Ania) but arouse in her merely platonic love. In Trofimov, sexuality is further diminished, for he recognizes only platonic love. Battling with ordinary sensuality, these "T" males all expound ideas of an extrasensory future, from Treplev's intimations of the world soul to Tuzenbakh's and Trofimov's speculation that humanity may have more than five senses.

Not all the cast of *The Cherry Orchard* reincarnate earlier Chekhovian characters. Lopakhin has no precedent on the Chekhovian stage, nor do the servants Duniasha and Iasha, who enact the roles of unrequited and unrequiting lovers that Chekhov previously assigned to his gentry. The alienated, casual characters Charlotta and Simeonov-Pishchik—the lost souls who play such a part in *The Cherry Orchard* and give the play such a sense of forlornness and "fatherlessness"—are innovations in Chekhov's work, even though Simeonov-Pishchik has in him a little of the *prizhival* ("hanger-on," "destitute neighbor") of Telegin in *Uncle Vania*. *The Cherry Orchard* extends from Chekhov's earlier plays the "one-off" importunate intruder, who appears only to declaim, to frighten, and to embarrass and then to vanish again. The passerby in act 2 and the station master in act 3 are extensions of the casual character, a tear in the weft of the plot rather than part of the tissue. The impression of disintegration, of what Osip Mandelstam called with withering scorn the "ecological" system of relating characters, thus becomes all the stronger.

The invisible members of the cast, however, loom as large in *The Cherry Orchard* as in Chekhov's other mature plays. Their determining role is revealed only in the course of the exposition. The dead—whether Ranevskaia's son, mother, and husband or Vera Petrovna, Uncle Vania's sister, or the father of the three sisters—predetermine whether the living are grounded in their estate or condemned to roam. The dead deprive the living of rights of accession. Chekhovian exposition is powerful, for it drops only hints about the past, leaving the rest for the spectator and reader to conjecture. How Grisha came to be drowned in the aftermath of Ranevskaia's husband's death, and whether Trofimov was to blame, is never revealed, just as the circumstances of Vera Petrovna's distress and death and her husband's guilt are left horribly unclear—just as the tyranny Colonel Prozorov exerted over his three daughters and what happened to their mother is never discussed, treated as a family tabu. The dead in Chekhov's work have sealed biographies. While Ibsen reveals all past shameful secrets dramatically, Chekhov tantalizingly withholds them from us. In earlier plays there are dark hints of illegitimacy, of putative paternity: Is Dr. Dorn the father of Masha in *The Seagull*? Is Dr. Chebutykin the father of Irina in *Three Sisters*? Clues are given, proof denied. *The Cherry Orchard*, where masculinity is vestigial, has no paternity. Nevertheless, mysterious figures exert power from offstage: Deriganov (who means to buy the orchard and who starts the auction), the aunt in Iaroslavl, and the lover in Paris are all unseen bearers of ill tidings, just as in *Three Sisters* Protopopov, Natasha's lover and Andrei's boss, manipulates the couple from behind the wings, or Nina's stepparents in *The Seagull* provoke her unhappy departure and return.

If Chekhov's cast seems to evolve a stereotype—a maladjusted, inadequate and unstable household—the subtitle "comedy" shows how much the playwright intended to distinguish his disintegrating family from the aura of classical tragic dynasties. Whatever her maternal defects, Ranevskaia is neither Clytemnestra nor Medea. It is significant that the first version (1887) of *Ivanov* (in which the eponymous hero dies of a heart attack at his second wedding) was subtitled "comedy." The censorship substituted "drama," a change Chekhov preserved in the definitive 1889 version, where Ivanov shoots himself. While the subtitle "comedy" is perfectly suited to the happy ending of *The Wood Demon*, Chekhov caused considerable shock when he insisted in using it for *The Seagull*, in which the young hero shoots himself and the young heroine is reduced to an Ophelia-like wreck, raving in a downpour or (in other interpretations) deprived of her innocence and turned into the same second-rate provincial actress as Arkadina. For a while Chekhov abandoned the term "comedy": *Uncle Vania* was just called "Scenes from Country

Intertextuality: Chekhov's Texts and The Cherry Orchard

Life" and *Three Sisters* a "drama," but the return to the subtitle "comedy" in *The Cherry Orchard* reinstates the norm.

The Cherry Orchard's similarities of plot and character to other Chekhov plays are matched by speeches that are not just typically "Chekhovian" but reminiscent in phrasing, particularly of *Uncle Vania*. Compare Trofimov's denunciation of the intelligentsia to Ania in act 2: "Most members of the intelligentsia, so far as I know it, are seeking nothing—they're still incapable of hard work. . . . They all philosophize away" with Astrov's denunciation of the provincial gentry to Sonia in act 2 of *Uncle Vania*: "All of them, all our good kind friends, have petty thoughts and feelings. They can't see further than the end of their nose." The transition from denunciation to personal appeal is managed in the same way. Trofimov tells Ania, "Every winter I'm hungry, sick and fearful, as poor as a beggar. The places where fate has driven me!" Similarly, Astrov complains, "I work—you know this—harder than anyone in the district, I'm ceaselessly pummelled by fate, I find life intolerably painful at times." Denunciation turning to complaint is a strategy of the male in act 2 of *The Seagull*—Trigorin enchants Nina with his lament, "and deal with it all I do, in haste, urged on and snapped at on all sides. I rush back and forth like a fox bayed by hounds"—and in act 2 of *Three Sisters* Vershinin seduces Masha with "Talk to your local intellectual. . . . [W]hy are his aspirations in life so low?" turning to "I'm seized with alarm, I'm racked by guilt." The function of the speech varies from emotional release to vapid verbalization, in proportion to the sexual input, but the conversational tactics are identical.

The lyricism of the active, dendrophiliac male, of Lopakhin admiring his own and nature's prospects—"Lord, you gave us immense forests, boundless plains, broad horizons" (act 2); "When my poppy was in bloom—what a picture"—takes up the speech of Astrov in *Uncle Vania*—"When I plant a birch tree and then see it green and swaying in the wind my heart fills with pride" (act 1)—and even of Tuzenbakh on the verge of death in act 4 of *Three Sisters*: "I look at these fir trees, at these maples and birches, and it's as if I'm seeing them for the first time in my life." The self-deceiving lyricism of the consoling female is even more akin. Ania's promise to her mother of a new cherry orchard—"lovelier still. . . . And your heart will be visited by joy"—repeats Sonia's improvised reassurance of the weeping Vania—"we shall see all this world's evil and all our sufferings drown in the mercy that will fill the earth"—and Olga's strenuous consolation of her two sisters: "our sufferings will turn to joy for those who live after us." Ranevskaia's repeated use of the nostalgic conjunction "If only . . ." (*esli by*) also echoes Olga, who ends *Three Sisters* with two utterances of *esli by*.

An extensive study of all Chekhov's plays can fully explore the ways in which certain basic linguistic strategies are repeated and varied in each successive play. It must be stressed that we are not talking about Chekhov's paucity of invention or a search for a better version of imperfect dialogue. What we are seeing is a new (very twentieth-century) interpretation in each play of the way in which human language fails to express thought, intention, and feeling. Chekhov's full-length plays, whether subtitled "comedy" or "drama," deal with human beings doomed to repeat themselves because they are unable to grapple verbally with their predicament.

If the trees are in fact the play's real protagonists—"characters" who do not lie and who suffer real death—then *The Cherry Orchard* takes to its logical extreme a factor in all Chekhov's plays since *The Wood Demon*: the destruction of the forests as the externalization of spiritual wasting in the articulate characters. This aspect of Chekhov's drama is demonstrated in the nonverbal elements in *The Cherry Orchard*. Here we need only point to the continuity between the trees that catch fire, or are threatened with being sold off, in *The Wood Demon*; Astrov's young trees that are trampled by the peasant cattle in the ecological disaster that envelops the action of *Uncle Vania*; the elm tree that dismays Nina in act 1 of *The Seagull*; the maple and the fir trees that Natasha decides to fell in act 4 of *Three Sisters*; and the massive destruction of the cherry orchard.

The fate of the trees is a real and symbolic element in the play that Chekhov naturally deals with more explicitly in narrative prose. To further our understanding of *The Cherry Orchard* we must turn to Chekhov's stories. We have shown that "Steppe" (1888) first made the association of act 1's cherry blossom with act 2's cemetery. Three other stories associated with Chekhov's journey to the south in the cherry blossom season of 1887 have some bearing on *The Cherry Orchard*. The years 1886–87 saw Chekhov at his most productive and varied, moving from stories commissioned to entertain a market to more original and personal narrative. No wonder that revising the stories of this transitional time for republication left its mark on the composition of *The Cherry Orchard*. Chekhov considered "Fortune," written straight after he returned from the South in June of 1887, one of his and his admirers' favorite stories, "a product of inspiration. A quasi symphony." "You struck me as a landscape artist," the painter Levitan assured him. The story has no plot: a shepherd and a forest warden converse on the steppe on a summer's night. The old shepherd, like Firs, remembers ominous noises like a rock humming before the emancipation of the serfs; he recalls the fear inspired by a sorcerer called Zhmenia, the forerunner of a murdered stranger that Firs recalls in the final scene of act 2 that was cut by Stanislavsky. They end by talking of buried treasure; then we find the "broken string" of *The Cherry Orchard*: "In the quiet air, scattering over the steppe, a sound passed. Something in the distance groaned dreadfully, struck a stone and ran over the steppe, going 'Takh, takh, takh.' When the sound died away, the old man looked inquiringly at Pantelei, who was standing unmoved, motionless. 'It's a bucket that's broken away in the mine shafts,' said the younger man after a moment's thought." "Fortune" ends like act 1 of *The Cherry Orchard*: dawn breaks, revealing the prehistoric grave-mounds around.

An anonymous reviewer singled out "Fortune" together with "Steppe" and other stories of 1887 as Chekhov's best work.[1] Two stories he mentions—"Tumbleweed" (or "Rolling Stone") and "Panpipes"—are the other progenitors of *The Cherry Orchard*. "Tumbleweed" embodies the narrative of Aleksandr Ivanych, a physically and mentally crippled outsider, a baptized Jew, in the tradition of the Russian "superfluous man." One of Ivanych's misfortunes expands on the significance of the noise of the breaking string:

> I was in some mines here in the Donets district. You've seen people being lowered into the seam itself. You remember, when the horse is got going and the wheel made to turn, then one bucket goes over the pulley into the seam and the other comes up. . . .

Well, I got into a bucket, I begin to go down and you can imagine, suddenly I hear "trrr." The chain has broken and I flew hellbound together with the bucket and the end of the chain. I fell eighteen feet on my chest and belly, while the bucket which was heavier fell before I did and I smashed this shoulder against the edge of it. . . . Now I cough constantly, my chest hurts and I have terrible psychological problems.[2]

"Panpipes" gives meaning to the musical effect at the end of act 1 of *The Cherry Orchard*: a farm manager is hunting with his dog and hears an old herdsman playing the panpipes: "in the thin whistle you could hear something harsh and extraordinarily full of yearning." The conversation that ensues is a lament for nature, despoiled and desiccated. This lament is, almost word for word, the foundation for Astrov's ecological lecture in act 3 of *Uncle Vania*: even the dialect expressions are identical. But the important message that follows the panpipes is the herdsman's conviction that the incompetence of the landowners and the death of the trees in this steppe country is a sign of perdition for the world (*miru gibel'*). But "Panpipes," 16 years before the play, summed up the ultimate significance of *The Cherry Orchard*: "You could sense the closeness of that unhappy and utterly inexorable time when the fields would become dark, the earth dirty and cold, when the weeping willow would seem even sadder . . . the highest note of the panpipes passed slowly [*protiazhno*, the same adverb that Chekhov uses for the noise of the breaking string] in the air and quivered, like the voice of a person weeping. The high note quivered, broke off, and the panpipes fell silent."

The prose of 1887 helps us to interpret the play, but many phrases and even incidents stem from earlier stories, although they anticipate characters' idiolect and are not so close to the core of *The Cherry Orchard*. Take, for instance, Lopakhin's volte-face. "An Unnecessary Victory" (1882) has a rich merchant buying up the library of the gentry he was supposed to be helping: "Despite all my wishes, I couldn't sell it any dearer." "Who bought it?" "I, Boris Peltser." Or take Gaev's boiled sweets ("They say I've wasted all my substance in fruit drops"). In its first printed version "Three Years" (1895) has the impoverished gentleman Panaurov, who "had spent his own and his wife's wealth and had big debts. They said of him that he had spent his fortune on food and lemonade." Countless minor elements in *The Cherry Orchard*, such as the allusion to A. K. Tolstoy's poem "The Scarlet Woman," also recur from earlier works. "The Literature Teacher" (1894) is rich in anticipations: the teacher-protagonist marries a girl whose parents own a large orchard full of "sweet cherries [*chereshnia*], apples, pears, wild chestnuts, eleagnus." He falls in love with her at a party, where they dance a *grande ronde* and the director of the town's credit union, who is known as the "mummy," would recite in a singsong voice "The Scarlet Woman."

"The Black Monk" (1894), one of Chekhov's most popular stories (it was translated into the major languages of Europe in his lifetime), holds a key to the interpretation of *The Cherry Orchard*. Although a Gothic, even sensational, tale of disease overtaking the psyche and body of a young intellectual, Kovrin, it also tells of the fall of a household and its remarkable orchard. The orchard belongs to the hero's father-in-law, Pesotsky, who runs his hyperbolic estate with autocratic mania. While the cherry orchard is a dream, this orchard is a nightmare: "In the big orchard . . . thick, black, corrosive smoke spread over the earth and, enveloping the trees, saved these thousands [of rubles] the frost. The trees stood there in chessboard pattern, the rows were straight and exact, like ranks of soldiers, and the pedantic exactness, the trees being the same height and with completely identical crowns and trunks, made the picture monotonous and even boring."[3] When Kovrin deserts his wife and the orchard is lost, we have a grimmer, more melodramatic variant of *The Cherry Orchard*. As Kovrin is about to die he reads a letter from his wife: "My father has just died. . . . Our orchard is perishing, alien people are in charge of it now, so that just what my poor father feared is happening." The plot of "The Black Monk" invites a political interpretation: the autocrat's orchard, which has no suitable heir, is an allegory of autocratic Russia; Kovrin, who abandons his heritage to ruin, is analogous to the radical intelligentsia. Kovrin is a better qualified intellectual than Trofimov, but their contempt for the orchard and their longing to flee from it are alike. "The Black Monk" validates the political subtext that interpreters have decoded in *The Cherry Orchard*.

Two stories, however, are genetically related to *The Cherry Orchard*. In "A Visit to Friends" (1898) Podgorin, a cold-blooded Moscow lawyer and friend of the Losev family, plays a part akin to Lopakhin's. He is invited to stay with the Losevs on their estate, which is now up for auction because of the father's debts and improvidence. Podgorin realizes after he arrives that Tatiana Loseva hopes he will marry her sister Nadezhda and thus bail out the family. After a moonlit scene in the garden, when Podgorin pretends not to be there, the encounter with Nadezhda is aborted, and using a flimsy pretext Podgorin flees to Moscow before dawn.

There are other similarities between "A Visit to Friends" and *The Cherry Orchard*. Looking at the lights of the railway line, Tatiana's friend Varia recites Nekrasov, as does the passserby in *The Cherry Orchard*. A little like Lopakhin, a little like Trofimov, Podgorin is left alone with Nadezhda while the other women watch, and he is invited to watch the moon rise in the garden. Nadezhda, like Ania, dreams of becoming an independent working woman; Podgorin, anticipating Lopakhin's phrase, tempts himself with, "Why not marry her, actually?" On their return to the house the merriment leads everyone to assume that the estate can be saved somehow: they even sing. The auction, Podgorin is told by the ne'er-do-well husband, Sergei Losev, is set for 7 August. In disgust, Podgorin goes back into the moonlit garden, which anticipates the setting of act 2 of *The Cherry Orchard*: instead of the wayside shrine we have an old tower "built in the times of serfdom," with fields, forest, birds singing in the distance, and, searching for Podgorin, the girl in white. Podgorin, like Trofimov, does not want love unless it is "a call to new forms of life, lofty and rational, on the eve of which we may be living and of which we sometimes have a premonition."

The story ends with Podgorin forgetting completely about the doomed household, but clearly Chekhov recycled Podgorin, stripping the authorial remoteness off the character and taking one aspect—the old professional friend of the family who disengages himself—for Lopakhin, and saving what remains—the puritanical fastidiousness—for Trofimov. But, if we assume that Sergei Losev is merely Ranevskaia's dead husband, the most striking resemblance between story and play lies in the heroine's appeal to the possible savior. Tatiana Loseva cries, "I swear to you by all that is sacred, by the happiness of my children, I cannot manage without Kuzminki! I was born here, this is my nest, and if they take it away from me, I shan't survive, I shall die of despair." Ranevskaia in act 3 tells Trofimov, "After all, I was born here, my father and mother lived here, my grandfather. . . . I love this house. Without the cherry orchard I can't make sense of my life, and if it really has to be sold, then sell me along with it."

The similarities between play and story are partly explicable by common source material—namely, the feckless letters from the Kiseliov family at Babkino, which Chekhov received from 1886 to 1900. "A Visit to Friends," where the male protagonist is still alive, is even closer than *The Cherry Orchard* to the biographical material at Chekhov's disposal. Perhaps because the story was closely linked to sordid details of a friend's life, Chekhov disowned it: it was published in a little known journal, *Cosmopolis*, and was the only mature work that Chekhov excluded from his collected works. (Although published in German in 1902, it was not republished in Russian until 1906.) Chekhov's virtual annihilation of the story is all a reason to recycle its material, even its phrases, for both *Three Sisters* and *The Cherry Orchard*.

After surrendering the manuscript of *The Cherry Orchard* to Stanislavsky, Chekhov published his last story, "The Bride." Here we see the author simultaneously using the same material in a story and a play, for in the summer of 1903 he was working, with the same agonizing care, on both. The story has affinities to *Three Sisters*: the heroine, in a northerly provincial town, is determined to escape to the metropolis from an Andrei who plays the violin and is about to become a civil servant. But the idea of escape from a family heritage, from a neurotic mother and a ruined garden, is much closer to *The Cherry Orchard*. The similarities are greatest when the heroine, Nadia, listens to the family's protégé, the tubercular intellectual Sasha, and takes his fantasies literally: the parallels with Ania and Trofimov are undeniable. The narrator's skeptical tone (which contemporary critics ignored) undermines the radical dream, just as effectively as does the comic structure and centrifugal dénouement of *The Cherry Orchard*.

"The Bride" opens in spring. Straightaway the visiting Sasha denounces the hypocrisies of the bourgeois household: "Early this morning I went into the kitchen and there were four servants sleeping on the floor, no bedsteads, just rags for bedding, stench, bedbugs, cockroaches. . . . Just like twenty years ago, no change."[4] Compare this with Trofimov in act 2 denouncing the household on whom he depends: "And right in front of their eyes the whole time there are workers living on filthy food and sleeping without pillows to their heads, thirty and forty to a room—and everywhere bugs, damp, stench and moral squalor."

"The Bride" is no comedy: Sasha is a sinister provocateur whom only death prevents from provoking other susceptible women to seek his cloud-cuckoo land. But Sasha's vision of the future incorporates the same utopian elements as Trofimov's. Sasha believes in an elite of "enlightened and sacred people" to create the kingdom of God on earth: "Little by little not a stone will be left standing of your town—everything will explode, everything will change, as if by magic. And there will then be enormous splendid houses here, extraordinary fountains, remarkable people." Compare this with Trofimov's "bright star that blazes from afar there," his "premonitions of happiness," and his belief that "all the things that are beyond [mankind's] reach will one day be brought close and made plain."

Nadia is inspired by the same restlessness as Ania, and the neglected town garden with its lilacs and sparkling dew and the ominously howling stove have the same effect on her imagination as the orchard and the premonitory noises on Ania's. Just as the approach of 22 August concentrates the tension of *The Cherry Orchard*, so the date of Nadia's impending wedding, 7 July, forces the action of "The Bride." The difference is that the story adumbrates a possible sequel to the play. The heroine, after abandoning the nest, goes off to study and returns merely to confirm that her flight was as wise as it was rash. But while her farewell is as naively final as Ania's—"Farewell, town," Nadia thinks, just as Ania calls out, "Farewell, old house! Farewell, old life!"—her escape may not be complete. Sasha's death leaves her to fend for herself intellectually, and the note of revolutionary, feminist optimism—"vivacious, cheerful, she abandoned the town"—is soured by just one typical Chekhovian phrase: "as she supposed." "The Bride" gives us a context by which to judge the authorial mood underlying, but excluded from, the play.

11

Intertextuality: Other Authors' Texts and *The Cherry Orchard*

For all its innovation, *The Cherry Orchard* embodies a great deal from Russian drama and certain elements from Russian narrative prose, from Russian classics and works by Chekhov's contemporaries. Through them and also directly we find important elements that derive from European literature, especially French and German. The play is thus not just a condensation of much Chekhov had written; it draws on the whole European tradition, which it proceeds to overthrow.

The obvious progenitor of Chekhovian drama in general and *The Cherry Orchard* in particular is the novelist Ivan Turgenev's best drama, *A Month in the Country*, written in 1849–50, first forbidden, then mutilated by censorship, and unperformed until the Moscow Arts Theater revived it at the beginning of this century. It has since been recognized as an innovative work, 40 years ahead of its time. Turgenev dismissed his drama as apprentice work for narrative prose. Despite its Chekhovian subtitle "comedy," *A Month in the Country* is a story-writer's play in a different sense than Chekhov's, for it lacks dramatic tension and the dialogue idly ambles in a novelistic way. While it is conventional—its dialogue gives explicit answers to direct questions, and it relies on clichés such as the resident German tutor and intrigues of the servants—Turgenev's play invents much that Chekhov was to use.

The central figure is Natalia, a bored wife, stuck on her estate for the summer, possibly the mistress of the cynical "friend of the house." She finds herself attracted to Beliaev, the young student whom she has employed to look after her son, Kolia. Here we have the preliminary Ranevskaia, Trofimov, and Grisha of *The Cherry Orchard*. Half-aware of her feelings, Natalia conspires to marry off to a middle-aged neighbor her 17-year-old ward, Verochka, who is a rival for Beliaev's affections. Verochka thus combines the situation of Varia and Ania in *The Cherry Orchard*. As in most of Chekhov's plays, this intrigue is observed and interpreted by the doctor. The ending of the "comedy" is, like that of *The Cherry Orchard*, quite uncomic: the young characters scatter, and there is no marriage, while the older characters keep their emotional and financial footing. While Natalia is no widow, her husband, Islaev, is almost superfluous to the action, and she is left alone with her self-deceiving sensuality. Of all the elements in Turgenev's play the theme of the irresponsible mother and stepmother link it most closely to *The Cherry Orchard*. The portrait of the young student and of the naive girl who falls for him is, as always in Turgenev, high in admiration and short on irony, but the unbridgeable moral and ideological generation gap between the two sets of characters anticipates the atmosphere of *The Cherry Orchard*.

Russia's only fully professional dramatist of note, Aleksandr Ostrovsky, had all the attention denied to Turgenev. His material—the merchant classes in collision with the gentry—appears to overlap with that of *The Cherry Orchard*. Ostrovsky's plays are often alluded to in Chekhov's drama, and the strong role of money—the girl without a dowry is a standard theme in Ostrovsky's tragedies and comedies—links Ostrovsky's plots to Chekhov's. One comedy, popular in Russia if not abroad, was *The Forest* (1870). Chekhov evidently bore it in mind when composing *The Cherry Orchard*. The central character is Gurmyzhskaia, a widow of 50, living respectably but with a louche metropolitan past, on her estate a few miles from town. She has a niece, Aksiusha, her ward, whom at first she plans to marry to another ward, a semi-educated youth, Bulanov. Her tyrannical treatment of her penniless niece and her own lusts for the youth are typically Ostrovskian material, and so are the coarse and cunning merchant Vosmibratov, to whom she sells parcels of forest when she needs money, and the ineffectual Petia, the merchant's son, whom Aksiusha loves. The dénouement is the conventional eighteenth-century deus ex machina: a traveling actor, Gurmyzhskaia's long-lost nephew, puts all to rights, so that both the young couple and Gurmyzhskaia and Bulanov can marry.

Like all Ostrovsky, it is an excellent vehicle for character actors, and it still has power to shock. Its effect on Chekhov is peripheral but marked. Gurmyzhskaia has Ranevskaia's sensuality and irresponsibility: as her neighbor Bodaev says in act 1, "If a woman wants to buy her lover a skullcap with a tassel, she sells well maintained timber forest to the first rogue she sees." Gurmyzhskaia loses receipts and contracts. Just as Ranevskaia tells Varia, so Gurmyzhskaia's niece Aksiusha is told that "nobody is forcing her" (*nikto ne nevolit / nevolit' ne budut—nevolit'* is an unusual verb). The same quotation from *Hamlet*, "Nymph, in thy orisons Be all my sins remembered," is used by Ostrovsky's actor-hero to dismiss the heroine and by Chekhov's Lopakhin to dismiss Varia. In the end, however, the forest that gives Ostrovsky his title no longer symbolizes nature devastated but a jungle in which predatory animals roam.

One other Ostrovsky play in which actors and acting play a key thematic part is *Talents and Admirers* (1881). It is feasible to see Petia Meluzov, a young student and teacher who tries to instill his idealism into the heroine, Negina, a naive, vulnerable actress, as a high-minded progenitor of Chekhov's Petia Trofimov at work on Ania. (As in Chekhov's *The Seagull*, Ostrovsky's *Talents and Admirers* lets the provincial theater vanquish the naive idealism.)

Chekhov strongly admired both Ostrovsky and contemporary playwrights who now seem prisoners of the conventions of the time. His letters speak enviously and without irony of the strong characterization and firm plotting of dramatists who now read as nonentities—for instance, Sergei Naidionov's *Deti Vaniushiny* (Vaniushin's Children) of 1902 and Vladimir Nemirovich-Danchenko's *Novoe delo* (New Business) of 1889. Many of them deal with superficially similar subjects—the decline of the old order (gentry or merchants), the bankruptcy of their businesses, and the alienation of children from their heritage. A trawl through Russian drama of the time brings up few plays with any striking resemblance to *The Cherry Orchard*. *Iskuplenie* (Redemption) was written in 1903 by Ignati Potapenko, a prolific and much-liked friend of Chekhov, who nevertheless satirized aspects of Potapenko as Trigorin in *The Seagull*. Potapenko's melodrama has a crazed family, the Sandalovs, squandering their inheritance on modish modern theater and coping with a feckless, debauched mother. It shows what *The Cherry Orchard* might have been without comedy.

A more Gothic melodrama of 1901, *Stary dom* (The Old House), by A. M. Fiodorov, has the Palauzovs—a landowner, Vladimir, and his young wife, Inna—returning to their neglected family estate and its inhabitants—a mad aunt, an old nanny, and the boyhood friend who now manages the estate. We first see the estate in half-light, with ghostly rustlings, mice scurrying about, and rusty locks. The estate has had no repairs for 25 years. The olfactory emphasis is Chekhovian: Inna says, "I can tell by the smell what an old house this is. Such a strange smell. Like a cemetery." In act 1, like Chekhov, Fiodorov has his heroine, Inna, exclaim, "So here's your nursery preserved with its table." The later acts have some Chekhovian touches: there are a lot of trees, including two old firs in act 3, but Gothic elements take over. From the mice we move to spiders, dead houseplants, starving peasants, and finally a "bluebeard's room" where love and death predominate. A girl has hanged herself, and in act 4 the mad aunt follows suit. Before this climax Inna and the estate manager fall in love and their betrayed spouses row violently. The play is valuable as a benchmark for the theatrical conventions Chekhov was waging war against.

Chekhov pays tribute to only one contemporary play: Gorky's *The Lower Depths* (1902). Set in a doss house, where a rebellious socialist, Satin, supplants a meek Christian, Luka, Gorky's play preaches revolution and denounces Tolstoyan submission. Satin's act 4 speech is a hymn to the collective spirit of man; he is more demagogic than Trofimov and intended by the author to be less vacuous: "Only man [*chelovek*] exists, everything else is the work of his hands and brain! Man! That's splendid. That sounds proud." When Trofimov takes up the topic of "the proud man" in act 2, he alludes to Gorky's firebrand. Several of the actors—including Chekhov's wife—in *The Cherry Orchard* had taken leading parts in *The Lower Depths*. Stanislavsky himself had played Satin, and quite apart from Chekhov's complex role as tutor, supporter, and antagonist to Gorky, the play (which had immediate success abroad, in Berlin) was inevitably very much in Chekhov's mind when he was composing his own drama.

Russian prose had been equally at home for the previous 50 years with the theme of decaying estates, but here the parallels with *The Cherry Orchard* are weaker than with such gruesome melodramas as Fiodorov's *The Old House*. Formalist critics who held that literature can only evolve by parody of the past point to the distortion of motifs from Turgenev's 1858 novel *Nest of Gentlefolk* in *The Cherry Orchard*. True, Turgenev's depraved antiheroine returns to the family estate from her lover in Paris, wrecking hopes of its redemption. The girl, Liza, who hoped to marry the activist hero, Lavretsky, retreats to a nunnery, and the middle-aged woman who has caused the disruption departs for her lover in St. Petersburg. There are also evocations of a dusty, abandoned house and a romantic garden at night. But the gap between Turgenev's fatalistic tragedy and Chekhov's comedy of free will abused is too wide to make the connection plausible.

It is Tolstoy's *War and Peace* that seems to provide a central symbol of *The Cherry Orchard*. In chapter 14 of part 1 of the epilogue, Tolstoy's "rough" hero, Pierre Bezukhov, anticipates the political crisis about to strike Russia after the apparent liberation from Napoleon. He warns his friend Nikolai, "While you stand waiting for the tightened string to break . . . everyone waits for the inevitable upheaval. . . . [P]eople should join hands to withstand the disaster." The link between the image of the breaking string and social disaster so exactly anticipates the sound of act 2 and Firs's reaction to it that we must suppose *War and Peace* to have been in Chekhov's mind—a conjecture confirmed by the extensive underlining in red that Chekhov had made in his copy of the novel.

Some contemporary works, however, show how topical Chekhov's subject matter was. One is a survey by a statistician of estates around the river Oka, 50 miles south of Moscow. I. P.

Intertextuality: Other Authors' Texts and The Cherry Orchard

Belokonsky's *Derevenskie vpechatleniia* (Country Impressions) of 1900 is full of harrowingly absurd touches that might occur in Chekhovian drama: a school teacher dies of pneumonia, a derelict park reminds the author "of the last judgment with its firs and pines," and the estate strikes him "as the Kingdom of the Dead." At another estate he is told that "the master came at night and left at night"; at another, where the master spends all his time taking the waters in foreign spas, he is asked, "Perhaps you'd like to buy it?"

While Chekhov's knowledge of his contemporaries' work in Russian was very wide, to judge by what he mentions and what little we know of his library (which was plundered by friends and visitors), his reading of foreign authors in the original or in translation was selective. His contacts with Moscow theaters gave him considerable knowledge of European theater, but few foreign plays can be credited with influencing the making of *The Cherry Orchard*. Indirectly, we might argue that Balzac's little-known 1848 play, *The Stepmother*, should be put at the head of the genealogy of Chekhov's last play. As the Russian critic Leonid Grossman pointed out, *The Stepmother*, shorn of melodramatic violence, provided Turgenev with the core for *A Month in the Country*.[1] Balzac shows a stepmother ruthlessly ridding herself of her rival—her stepdaughter—by marrying her off to an older man. Turgenev borrowed even the phrasing of the play and can be said to have passed on to Chekhov the ambiguous manipulation of the younger by the older woman, of Varia by Ranevskaia. We may thus infer that Ranevskaia's feelings for Trofimov and Lopakhin, like Balzac's Gertrude for Ferdinand and Turgenev's Natalia for Beliaev, are tinged with impropriety.

Chekhov is today classed as the final crest of the "new wave" that allowed drama to reconquer its predominance from opera in European theatres. This is why he is discussed in the same breath as Ibsen, Strindberg, Shaw, and Gerhart Hauptmann. But there is little to be found in his plays that reflects communion with the other "new" dramatists. Ibsen he read and, on the whole, disliked: the title of *The Seagull* parodies Ibsen's *The Wild Duck*, and the suicide of Treplev after the destruction of his manuscripts seems more a pastiche of than a tribute to Ejlert Løvborg's suicide after Hedda Gabler burns his manuscript. The Chekhovian male with "vine leaves in his hair" is unimaginable, and women with far less atavism than Hedda Gabler can control him. Those who read Ibsen in Norwegian find the same subtle use of idiolect to characterize each role, as in Chekhov—a device that the unstable state of Norwegian then allowed the dramatist. Ibsen's language, however, is conventional in the expressive power it gives the characters and the use of interrogation, revelation, asides, and sotto voce. The most obvious common element in "new" drama is the newfound dominance of the female over weak-willed males. It can be traced to the sad fantasies of Leopold Sacher-Masoch, whose play *Unsere Sklaven* (Our Slaves), very popular in Russia in the late 1870s, portrays a world of female newspaper editors, political éminences grises, who torment their male secretaries and treat men as "just our slaves."[2] In Ibsen, Strindberg, and Chekhov the reversal of established sexual hierarchies is part of a theme affecting European philosophy and literature from Schopenhauer and Turgenev to D. H. Lawrence.

Only one "new" playwright appears to be specifically involved in *The Cherry Orchard*. Gerhart Hauptmann's *Lonely People* (1891) has curious and inexplicable Chekhovian touches, since Hauptmann (although in touch with cultural events in Russia) could not have read *Ivanov*. Hauptmann's hero, Johannes Vockerat, suffering the same depression as Ivanov and irritated by the same cynical boon companion, abandons a loving wife for an outsider (a Russian citizen, Anna Mahr) and then commits suicide. The connection is reversed when Chekhov writes *The Seagull*, and this time we know that he had read Hauptmann. *Lonely People* is echoed in Treplev's intellectual failure, his ill-requited love for an independent-minded heroine, his suicide, and the haunting presence of a lake throughout both plays. Together with *Hedda Gabler, Lonely People* was one of the most controversial productions in the repertoire of the Moscow Arts Theater in 1900–1901. Olga Knipper played Anna Mahr; few plays are mentioned so frequently in Chekhov's letters. One touch is borrowed for *The Cherry Orchard*: in act 1, at a baptism, the servant Minna, like Duniasha, casts a pall on the celebrations by breaking crockery.

We have seen how ambiguously Chekhov was received by Russian symbolists. In their work, particularly Blok's lyrical drama, there is a deceptively similar common ground: they deal with human beings who are drained of emotion, who have helpless aspirations and inhabit unreal, dreamlike worlds. Russian symbolism was much more directly connected with its French and Belgian teachers than with Chekhov, however. Symbolists appreciated Chekhov only where he coincides with Western symbolism. Ever since Meierkhold first took issue with a realistic approach to *The Cherry Orchard*, Maurice Maeterlinck has been cited as a precedent, even an antecedent, for Chekhovian drama. The play most often singled out is the one-act *Intérieur* (Interior) of 1894. It opens in an old garden planted with willows, with a group of characters, a stranger, an old man and his two granddaughters, watching and discussing an interior: a silent, doll-like nuclear family in their sitting room. The old man has news to impart: one of the family has just died. The audience watch but do not hear the family's reaction. Trees, garden, the menace that is realized, the long pauses, and the echoing phrases do in fact faintly anticipate Chekhov, but Maeterlinck's lugubrious, pretentious atmospherics are techniques Chekhov parodied in *The Seagull* and have little to do with his own use of otherworldly sensations and stylized speech in *The Cherry Orchard*. Although modern drama owes as much—the use of highly stylized repetitive and poetic utterance—to Maeterlinck's limited talent as to Chekhov's genius, the threads to Chekhovian absurdity and to Maeterlinckian atmospherics have to be traced separately. All that links *The Cherry Orchard* with Maeterlinck's drama is a common funereal fondness for stage afforestation.

The more conventional French drama of the day has even slighter relevance to Chekhov's work: it is worth mentioning just one highly regarded play of 1882, Henri Becque's *The Crows* (or *The Vultures*). The corpse of a good-natured father is carried across the stage at the end of act 1, one daughter goes mad, and another has to prostitute herself to the business partner who robs the family, but *The Crows* is subtitled "comedy"—proof that Chekhov's morbid use of the term and the genre was not unprecedented. *The Crows* shows a group of women—a naive, incompetent widow; her three daughters; and the governess—losing their family fortune to a ruthless conspiracy of men—a businessman, a lawyer, and an architect whom they had assumed to be their friends and saviors. On the surface *The Crows* appears to be Chekhovian material—the widow unable to find any documents, the youngest daughter, Blanche, trusting (until she is deranged) to love and human charity. But Henri Becque is a hybrid of Dumas fils and Ibsen, of bourgeois sentiment and of classical ruthlessness, and his taut, logical construction of forlorn material is utterly un-Chekhovian.

One classic European play, however, underlies most of Chekhov's work, as it does most of Russian literature: Shakespeare's *Hamlet*. It is Hamlet's impotent rejection of Ophelia that inspired so many poets—from Afanasi Fet to Marina Tsvetaeva and Boris Pasternak—and prose writers such as Turgenev and Chekhov. Lopakhin's misquotation of Hamlet's "Get thee to a nunnery" and "Ophelia! Nymph and in thy orisons Be all my sins remember'd" point out to a Russian audience his feet of clay, that he suffers from Hamlet's incapacity for love. The Hamletian atmosphere is not as overt as in *The Seagull*, where Treplev and Arkadina reenact the scenes between Hamlet and Gertrude, from the staging of a provocative play to the accusations of fornication. But Chekhov's theme of the inadequate mother—and of "The Scarlet Woman"—remains linked to Shakespeare's Gertrude.

As in *Three Sisters*, however, another Shakespeare play overshadows *The Cherry Orchard*: we detect *Macbeth* in the subtext, and the echoes are unmistakable, though subconscious. Both plays have 20 references to sleeplessness or sleep; both are full of breakages, ghosts, birds, and trees of good and evil omen; both have an ill-starred banquet and a disastrously dominant heroine upsetting the balance of cast and the action. Both are plays in which trees are pro-active: Birnam wood prefigures the cherry orchard. Chekhov's comedy mirrors Shakespeare's tragedy: in *Macbeth* tragedy ensues from the Macbeths' determination to see a prediction of power come true, while in *The Cherry Orchard* comedy ensues from Gaev and Ranevskaia's refusal to see a prediction of financial ruin fulfilled.

It has even been suggested that another European classic appropriated by Russian literature, Goethe's *Faust*, plays a part in shaping *The Cherry Orchard*.[3] Certainly in 1902 Chekhov mentions in letters that he was reading new prose translations of both *Hamlet* and *Faust*. We also find in the broken clock of *Three Sisters* an echo of the broken clock in *Faust*. Act 5 of part 2 opens with a wanderer returning to a lime tree grove where the elderly owners, Philemon and Baucis, bemoan the destruction of their grove to make way for the canal that Faust and Mephistopheles are building (it is in fact to be Faust's grave). Gaev and Ranevskaia are as implausible a Philemon and Baucis, and Lopakhin is an unlikely Faust, but the parallel between the lime grove and the cherry orchard is visible, if inconsequential.

There is but one unquestionable European source for *The Cherry Orchard*, and that is Maupassant's *A Life* (1883). Maupassant is the dominant influence in Chekhov's prose and in several plays. *The Seagull* has Dr. Dorn reading from Maupassant's travel reflections, *Sur l'eau* (On the Water), and Treplev approving Maupassant's horror of the vulgar Eiffel Tower; the play's opening lines—"Why do you always wear black?" "I'm in mourning for my life"—distill the conversation of the abandoned Mme Walter and Madeleine in Maupassant's novel *Bel-Ami*. *The Cherry Orchard* is likewise indebted to *A Life*, where, as in Chekhov's play, the noble widow of a debauchee is forced to sell her family estate to an agricultural businessman. The estate is not a cherry orchard, but it is called "the poplars" (*les peuples*, Norman dialect for *peupliers*). In chapter 12 of *A Life* Maupassant's heroine reacts to the sale with the same horror as Ranevskaia: "Jeanne suddenly sat up in bed: 'Sell The Poplars! How can you think of it? Oh, never, really!'" Her farewell to the garden, saturated with memories of her mother, has the same sentimental extravagance as Ranevskaia's reaction to the orchard: "Then until evening she walked all alone up and down her mother's avenue, her heart broken, her spirit distressed, addressing desperate, sobbing farewells to the horizon, to the trees, to the worm-eaten bench under the plane tree, to an old decapitated elm she had often leant against, to the whole familiar garden."

Maupassant's short novel significantly differs from Chekhov in characters: the heroine is naively prudish, rather than improvident; the love that blinds her is not erotic love but the love for her dissipated son; the story is peopled with peasants and priests, not intellectuals. The atmosphere, characteristically for Maupassant and Chekhov's prose, is imbued with the sea. But Maupassant, unlike Chekhov, cannot deny the reader a violent climax and morally uplifting end. The detailed resemblances between *A Life* and Chekhov's play are, nevertheless, backed up by thematic parallels: Maupassant is dealing with a last generation of the gentry, doomed by their incomprehension of money, with the dissolute males squandering family fortunes and neglecting patrimony, the estate. He too uses the device of the faithful old servant taking charge of infantile master or mistress. Maupassant is the only modern European writer whose work substantially shaped *The Cherry Orchard*.

12

The Aftermath

The first, most explicit, and perhaps the most viable aftermath of *The Cherry Orchard* in world literature was Bernard Shaw's *Heartbreak House* of 1919, subtitled "A Fantasia in the Russian Manner on English Themes." Shaw's Preface, as usual nearly as long as the play and sometimes wittier and more enthralling, emphatically avows his debt to Chekhov. Building on his unpopular advocacy of *The Cherry Orchard* in England seven years before, he now identifies his characters with Chekhov's: "helpless wasters of their inheritance." Shaw's very politicized condemnation of the Ranevskaia-Gaev household may seem an overly judgmental interpretation of Chekhov's subtle authorial hints, but it does not lessen the Chekhovian influence on the play. Shaw keeps up his typical pursuit of the witty generalization and sharp repartee, which allies him more to Oscar Wilde than to Chekhov. While his humor strains for the outlandish, it is always grounded on maxim and aphorism, which play a minor role in Chekhov. Shaw attempts to shock rather than bewilder his audience with the irresponsibility of his characters. *Heartbreak House* is all the more interesting for being the effort of a profoundly un-Chekhovian author to use Chekhovian structures for purposes of denunciation and propaganda more akin to those of Maksim Gorky.

In Shaw's view, "Heartbreak House" is the England of ineffectual talk, as opposed to "Horseback Hall," which is the England of insensitive, inarticulate action. Both, his Preface asserts, have led England into World War I and social catastrophe. The play, however, is concerned only with the first half of English society, symbolized by a house dominated by the eccentric and aged Captain Shotover, whose ruthless opinions and uninhibited behavior ally him very much to the Chekhovian doctor. Shotover represents the God-like author, whom Chekhov has so carefully absented from his last play. Shaw's plot is based, as so often in his work, around an articulate, free-thinking young woman, Ellie, who will manipulate and marry to achieve the freedom that poverty and men deny her. She is invited to Heartbreak House by one of the Shotover daughters, Hesione Hushabye, whose main interest, despite the critical state of the household, is arranging or disarranging unions between the men and women she dominates. The crisis around the house builds up until the final third act, where the noise of bombers signals the destruction of the house and the store of dynamite Captain Shotover keeps in a gravel pit explodes: the play ends with two dead and the rest reveling in imminent extinction.

The relationship of the bombs and dynamite to Lopakhin's ax is only too explicit. Equally Chekhovian is the union between the impoverished Miss Ellie and the middle-aged "captain of industry," Boss Mangan, based on mutual interest not love, which is eventually abandoned when Ellie goes through a form of marriage with Captain Shotover. This plot element, added to the revelation of Mangan's weakness—he can be hypnotized, made to weep, and admit how insubstantial his confidence and his wealth are—is clearly generated by Chekhov's Varia-Lopakhin plot. Ellie, in her apparent naivety and loyalty, also contains elements of Ania. Chekhov's Ranevskaia, however, is split by Shaw into the two Shotover married daughters, Hesione Hushabye and Ariadne Utterword. Like Ranevskaia, Ariadne has returned home after a long stay abroad; both are free-thinking to the point of libertinage and control the men in their sway with the virtuosity of Ranevskaia. It is, however, Hesione who recalls Ranevskaia: "a gorgeous woman," "siren," "coaxing, kissing, laughing" are Shaw's attributes for her. Other characters are less flagrantly Chekhovian. The idealist Mazzini Dunn, Ellie's father, is, like Trofimov, called a prig by his sensuous hostess. Hector Hushabye, the compliant husband, has the same obsessive patterns of behavior (Munchausen fantasies, rather than empty speechifying) as Gaev, while the old nurse, Guinness, with her scorn for the new world, fills much the same function as Firs. Chekhov's intruders who add only disquiet to the plot are matched by Shaw's burglar.

Shaw's political vehemence distinguishes him from Chekhov, but much of what Shotover preaches is to be heard from Chekhov's idealists: "Go, Boss Mangan," says the captain, evoking the joys of unbounded seas and skies as opposed to the confines of the house in terms very like Trofimov urging Ania to leave the orchard. And just as "Let's go" is heard at the conclusion of each act of *The Cherry Orchard*, so here we have an order to go that is never acted on until it is too late. The ineffectuality of the characters is summed up by Shaw: "We do not live in this house: we haunt it"—a phrase that perfectly fits *The Cherry Orchard*, so haunted by ghosts. One might also argue Shaw's dislike of sexuality—"Any slavery on earth than this slavery of men to women!"—is Chekhovian, were it not that the males of *The Cherry Orchard* are too lacking in libido to be enslaved by sex: the Chekhovian male is paralyzed more by absolute absence of will.

Heartbreak House is perhaps more Chekhovian in intent than reality. Shaw's reaction when he attended a performance of his play by students in Oxford in the 1920s shows that he continued to understand Chekhov in his own way: the students played *Heartbreak House* as a farce, thereby annoying Shaw, who insisted that it was to be a "half-tragedy, like Chekhov."

German theater also reacted to the first impact of *The Cherry Orchard* with an attempt to add to its genre. Lion Feuchtwanger's "melancholic" 1921 comedy, *Der Amerikaner, oder die entzauberte Stadt* (The American; or, The Disenchanted City), the author excluded from his collected works and thus made a bibliographical rarity. The comedy is a pastiche of Chekhov: Filippo, the Lopakhin-like son of an innkeeper, returns from America to the south of Italy to buy the estate, the *borgo*, of the feckless Marchese and his daughter Beatrice, who have roles comparable to those of Gaev and Ranevskaia. The

Marchese, whose heart is in Paris, we are told, "is not meant for the ordinary world. When people talk of business he sniffs as if something smelt bad." Act 3 is spent waiting for the results of an election, on which the mortgage, and thus the fate, of the estate depends. Filippo unexpectedly stands, wins against the Marchese, and takes over the *borgo*. In act 4, however, he is more merciful than Lopakhin: he abandons plans to build a hotel and sardine factory and begins to restore the ruined palace, although the aristocrats still take the train for the big city. There are many other reminiscences of Chekhov: a shepherd's bagpipes end the first and final acts; Georg von Weber, a German romantic, enchants the young heroines with his Romantic speculations; and the innkeeper's daughter is in love with a boastful, Yasha-like soldier Ettore. Act 2 is dominated by overgrown conifers (yews instead of cypresses), and the Marchese is obsessed by his coin collection. This "melancholic" comedy is a gentler, less witty, and more whimsical variant of *The Cherry Orchard*. Feuchtwanger was more competent as an assistant translator than as an imitator of Chekhov. The failure of would-be Chekhovian comedy is significant for the direction that German theater took, as was Rilke's abandonment of Chekhovian drama for lyrical poetry. Brechtian drama, a more carnival, propagandist genre, swept the ineffectual "theater of mood" off the German stage.

In Soviet Russia, nothing was more alien to the "new theater," under the sway of epic cinema and the needs of propaganda, than Chekhovian drama. Parallels have been noted between Mikhail Bulgakov's valediction to the gentry—his dramatization of his novel *The White Guard*, known as *The Days of the Turbins*—but the two doctor-writers have very different senses of nostalgia and irony. Bulgakov was in any case indifferent to Chekhov's work. Bulgakov's second wife, however, recalls him devising a sketch called "White Clay," which was to improvize on the theme of the white clay found on Simeonov-Pishchik's land, making him rich in act 4 of *The Cherry Orchard*: the sketch is lost.

If we dismiss the efforts of "English Chekhovians" and turn to drama of our day, we may find that fragments of *The Cherry Orchard* can be retrieved from what appears to be a wholly different conception of theater, based on nightmares, interrogations, and primitive rites. Yet Samuel Beckett, for example, had a reticence about the role of the author, which is worded in the same terms as Chekhov: "I am not a philosopher. One can only speak of what is in front of him, and that is simply a mess," Beckett is reported to have said in 1961.[1] This strongly echoes Chekhov's belief that a writer practicing philosophy was as wicked as a layman practicing medicine, or his letter of 1888 to Suvorin, in which he wrote, "It's time writers, especially artists, admitted that you can't make anything out in this world. . . . If an artist trusted by the mob decides to declare that he understands nothing of what he sees, that will make at least one piece of knowledge in the realm of thought" (No. 447). Ideological minimalism is the real link between *The Cherry Orchard* and Beckett's drama.

While there is some truth in analogies between Beckett's and Chekhov's views of the theater as a "black pit" threatening the actor, most comments on the relationship of late Chekhovian drama to Beckett's work center, however, on three other areas. First, an audience can leave the play with the conviction that nothing has happened. Second, we can compare remorseless authorial pessimism seeping through the idiotic optimism of a character. In this sense the immobilized but cheerful Winnie of *Happy Days* (1961) is a remote but recognizable descendant of Ranevskaia. Third, we can understand the Chekhovian utterance, in the mouth of Gaev, Ranevskaia, or Trofimov, as being a desperate tissue of language to disguise the emptiness of their being, so that Chekhov's lyrical, improvised rhetoric can be seen as a proto-language for the remorseless, fantastical logic of Beckett's characters. But there are other ways in which Beckett seems specifically to continue Chekhov's symbolism of the eloquent but betrayed cherry trees. The stage setting of *Waiting for Godot* (1955) is dominated throughout the play by a gaunt, leafless tree, which comes to life a little, by growing a few leaves for act 2, but yet fails to inspire the two tramps with the determination to hang themselves. (Note that *Waiting for Godot* is designated a "comedy" and that its sole indication of the set is the minimally Chekhovian "A country road. A tree.") So dominant is the tree symbol in *Waiting for Godot* that the prison walls of *Endgame* (1958) or the sandy, post-Holocaust landscape of *Happy Days*, Beckett's later plays, make the tree conspicuous by its absence.

Beckett, like Chekhov, forgets the conventional dramatist's inhibition about drawing attention to the passage of time. Pozzo looks at his watch and measures time past and future with the same obsessiveness as Lopakhin. In *Endgame* the perpetual Chekhovian question "What time is it?" now gets the answer it deserves: "The same as usual." In *Waiting for Godot* the strange antics of Pozzo with his cold chicken and pipe, or Estragon and the radish, expand the absurdity of Charlotta's cucumber, Iasha's smell of chicken and cigars. Beckett is hardly Chekhovian, but he evolves many elements of Chekhov in general and *The Cherry Orchard* in particular.

One might see (but not in a production that uses Stanislavsky's additional directions) a premonition of Beckett in the last moments of act 3 of *The Cherry Orchard*, where Ania repeatedly begs her mother, the pole-axed Ranevskaia, "We'll go away, we'll go away. . . . Come, come!" (all four verbs are the same in the original: *poidiom*), and yet Chekhov gives no stage direction to indicate that Ranevskaia should move. At the end of *Waiting for Godot* Vladimir and Estragon decide to go away to return to test fate the next day: "Well? Shall we go?" "Yes, let's go." But Beckett directs, *They do not move.* Chekhov's close of each act is particularly Beckett-like, and the final entry of Firs could be held to be the primary sources of all Beckett's senile Everymen.

The absurd, surreal, or cruel French theater with which Beckett is associated has far more tenuous links with *The Cherry Orchard*. Nevertheless, Chekhov's last play was recognized by them to be, like Strindberg's drama, their predecessor in abandoning realism in speech and direct representation of reality. When Antonin Artaud, one of the most influential theoreticians and practitioners of the "theater of cruelty," proclaimed the death of the old theater in the 1931 lecture "Staging and Metaphysics" (later included in his violent manifesto, *Le Théâtre et son double*), he had in mind *The Cherry Orchard* as a specimen of the new theater: "I am well aware that the language of gestures and poses, dance, music are not so good as verbal language at elucidating character, narrating a person's human thoughts, setting out clear and precise states of consciousness, but who said that theatre was made to elucidate character, solve conflicts that involve human passions, contemporary affairs or psychology, such as fill our theaters today?"

Gaev's phantom game of billiards that counterpoints speech and action and displaces emotion is raised to the dominant theme in Arthur Adamov's more didactic and politicized than "absurd" *Le Ping-Pong* of 1955, which is inspired by the billiard halls of the Mabillon in Paris. Adamov, himself of Russian-Armenian origin, was all the more vulnerable to the influence of *The Cherry Orchard* since his first steps as a dramatist came after contact with Georges Pitoëff, the first French producer of Chekhov, and he had himself translated much of Chekhov's dramatic work. Adamov's drama—surreal or semi-real—shows characters as victims of fatal historical processes that they cannot comprehend or address, but political commitment make his hostility to capitalism quite a different motive force for the plays: there is no authorial ambiguity.

At the time of this writing, when ecological themes and the "rape of the landscape" obsess us, *The Cherry Orchard* has taken on new life. The American *Foxfire* of 1979, by Susan Cooper and Hume Cronyn, and an English BBC radio play of 1992, John Fletcher's *The Apple Orchard*, are convincing evidence of renewal. *Foxfire* deals with an ancestral farm, whose owner, Annie, finds selling inconceivable. Annie is fixed on thoughts of her dead husband and cannot listen to the advice of an estate developer. In the end she leaves to join her son, and her husband, like Firs, haunts the empty stage. The Chekhovian humor and poetry is gone, but the Appalachian setting gives the skeleton of the play some life.

The Apple Orchard, broadcast in March 1992 but originally conceived for the stage, is a rare example of a pastiche that inherits the strengths of its model. Set in an England of the future, after a nuclear holocaust and the collapse of the international economy, *The Apple Orchard* has a brother and sister, Jonathan and Isabelle Johnson, returning with enormous difficulty, after 20 years in London, to the gas station in rural Somerset, where they grew up. Here they find their half sister Sam living with the rustic manager of the station, Harold

Golledge, visited by an eccentric vicar, who is also a nuclear scientist responsible for the derelict power station nearby. Offstage is Sam's baby and the senile, dying father of the Johnsons. These characters condense Chekhov's cast by half: Jonathan and Isabelle retain most of the features of Gaev and Ranevskaia, but Sam is Varia, Ania, and Trofimov rolled into one. Harold Golledge plays their friend and enemy Lopakhin (and in his wisdom incorporates elements of Firs), while the vicar is an expanded Simeonov-Pishchik. The white concrete of the gas station, all that is left of the Johnsons' business empire, is forlorn—there are almost no more cars and the only fuel is distilled cider. Harold, the vicar, and the local parish council plan to dig up the concrete forecourt and plant an apple orchard.

The Apple Orchard thus reverses the destruction of *The Cherry Orchard*. Despite Jonathan and Isabelle's refusal to countenance the change, at a crucial meeting offstage Harold and the vicar force the purchase on them. Sam steals the carburetor from her brother's car and flies off in her home-made airplane to a women's commune on the magic Hebridean island of Iona. The impoverished vicar has borrowed marijuana from Jonathan (the only currency left in England is drugs); he becomes rich when he finds magic mushrooms on his land. Repaid in mushrooms, Jonathan and Isabelle can escape to the coast, to England's last flourishing port, to restore capitalism with their mushroom currency and to find Isabelle's lost demonic lover. They leave Harold to administer care to the baby and euthanasia to the patriarch.

Whole passages of *The Cherry Orchard* are grafted with great skill into John Fletcher's vision of catastrophe, which, for all its English jokes and "New Age" whimsy, brings out what is universal in Chekhov's last play and what we can appreciate even more than Chekhov's contemporaries: the fragility of the earth's ecology and the endurance of human stupidity and cupidity. *The Cherry Orchard* has probably yet to reveal its full potential.

Notes

2. The Importance of *The Cherry Orchard*

1. Radical drama in Russia included Aleksandr Blok's *Neznakomka* (1908; The Stranger); Western European examples include George Bernard Shaw's *Heartbreak House* (1919) and Samuel Beckett's *Waiting for Godot* (1954; in French, 1952).

2. Søren Kierkegaard, *(Concluding) Unscientific Postscript* (London: Oxford University Press, 1954), 81.

3. Critical Reception

1. Konstantin Stanislavsky, telegram to Chekhov, 21 October 1903.

2. Maria Lilina, letter to Chekhov, 18 October 1903.

3. Vladimir Nemirovich-Danchenko, telegram to Chekhov, 21 October 1903.

4. A. L. Vishnevsky, letter to Chekhov, undated [November 1903].

5. See Osip Dymov, "Pervoe predstavlenie Vishniovogo sada v Sankt-Peterburge," *Utro Rossii* 4 (1904): 1.

6. See Vladimir Nemirovich-Danchenko, *Iz proshlogo*, vol. 1 (Moscow: Iskusstvo, 1952), 177.

7. Vladimir Nemirovich-Danchenko, telegram to Chekhov, 2 April 1904.

8. Nemirovich-Danchenko, *Iz proshlogo*, 1: 107.

9. Aleksandr Amfiteatrov, *Rus'* [newspaper], no. 110, 31 March 1904; no. 111, 1 April 1904.

10. See Zinaida Gippius, *Novy Put'* [St. Petersburg journal] 5 (1904): 251–67.

11. See Zinaida Gippius, *Novy Put'* [St. Petersburg journal] 8 (1903): 184–87.

12. Vlas Doroshevich, *Russkoe Slovo* [St. Petersburg newspaper], no. 19, 1904.

13. Andrei Bely, *Arabeski* (Moscow: Skepion, 1911), 400.

14. Vsevolod Meierkhold, letter to Chekhov, 8 May 1904; see *Literaturnoe Nasledstvo* [Moscow] 68 (1960): 448.

15. Vsevolod Meierkhold, "Teatr. K istorii i tekhnike," in *Teatr. Kniga o novom teatre* (St. Petersburg: Shipovnik, 1908), 143.

16. Maksim Gorky, *Sobranie sochineii v 30i tomax*, vol. 28 (Moscow: Nauka, 1954), 291.

17. Viktor Baranovsky, letter to Chekhov, 20 March 1904, RGB Archives.

18. M. Khosidov, letter to Chekhov, 13 June 1904, RGB Archives.

19. Ivan Bunin, *O Chekhove* (New York: Chekhov Publishing House, 1955), 216.

20. Osip Mandelstam, *Sobranie sochinenii*, vol. 4 (Paris: YMCA Press, 1981), 108–109.

21. Viacheslav Pietsukh, *Ia i prochee* (Moscow, 1990), 42.

22. For example, London *Daily Telegraph*, no. 21, 1911; see Victor Emeljanow, *Chekhov: The Critical Heritage* (London: Routledge & Kegan Paul, 1981), 10–11.

23. Maurice Baring, "Russian Literature," *New Quarterly* [London] 1 (1907–1908): 405-29.

24. George Bernard Shaw, quoted by H.M.W. in the *Nation* [London], 16 May 1914, 265–66.

25. Virginia Woolf, in Emeljanow, *Critical Heritage*, 200.

26. Frank Swinnerton, in Emeljanow, *Critical Heritage*, 192.

27. Storm Jameson, "Modern Dramatists," *Egoist*, 16 March 1914, 116–17.

28. Anonymous reviewer, *Dramatist* 4 (July 1915): 590–91.

29. Edmund Wilson, "The Moscow Arts Theatre," *Dial* 74 (January 1923): 319.

30. Brooks Atkinson, "The Cherry Orchard," *New York Times*, 11 March 1928, pt. 8, p. 1.

31. Tyrone Guthrie, in Emeljanow, *Critical Heritage*, 380.

32. Miss Le Gallienne, in Emeljanow, *Critical Heritage*, 441.

33. James Agate, Sunday *Times* [London], 31 May 1925.

34. *Daily Express*, quoted by Patrick Miles, *Chekhov on the British Stage, 1909–1987* (London: Sam and Sam, 1987), 26.

35. Lion Feuchtwanger, "Der Kirschgarten," *Die Schaubühne* [Munich] 33 (1916): 175–182.

36. Letter to Olga Knipper, in *Polnoe sobranie sochinenii i pisem v 30i tomakh* (Moscow: Nauka, 1974–83), letter nos. 4214 and 4238. Letters from these volumes are hereafter cited in text by number.

37. Arthur Adamov, *Ici et maintenant* (Paris: NRF, 1969), 197.

38. Jean-Louis Barrault, "Pourquois *La Cerisaie?*" in *Cahiers de la Compagnie Madeleine Renard–Jean-Louis Barrault* (Paris: Gallimard, 1954), 87–97.

4. The Making of the Text

1. See M. P. Chekhova, *Pis'ma k bratu* (Moscow, 1954), 124.

2. "Steppe," in *Polnoe sobranie sochinenii i pisem v 30i tomakh: sochineniia*, vol. 7 (Moscow: Nauka, 1985), 14; volume hereafter cited as *PSS*.

3. Unpublished, in the Russian State Library Archives, 331, 32.

4. Like Michael Frayn, I, too, am unconvinced by the editorial notes to volume 11 of *PSS* (1986, 396–98), where it is argued that the surviving text of the play we used to know as *Platonov* (adapted by Frayn as *Wild Honey*) is in fact the unpublished play under the title *Bezotsovshchina* (Fatherlessness). I doubt it because "fatherlessness" plays no part in the themes or plot of the play.

5. Mark Aldanov, preface to Bunin, *O Chekhove*, 18.

6. Aleksei Sergeevich Kiseliov, quoted in *PSS*, 13: 482.

7. Maria Kiseliov, quoted in *PSS*, 13: 482.

8. Chekhov, letter to A. S. Suvorin, 30 May 1888, No. 447.

9. Nikolai Leikin, recalled by Mikhail Pavlovich Chekhov, *Vokrug Chekhova* (Moscow: Moskovsky rabochii, 1960), 207–208.

10. Chekhov's notebooks quoted from *PSS*, 17: 9.

11. Chekhov first wrote down the word *nedotiopa* (a gem that even Dal's great dictionary does not list but that in *The Cherry Orchard* is part of the household idiolect) in a 13 August 1893 letter to his girlfriend, Lika Mizinova: "The *nedotiopa* Ivanenko is the same old nedotiopa and treads on roses, mushrooms, dogs' tails etc." (No. 1333). The word appears in the Chekhov's notebooks in 1902: "On his cross someone wrote 'Here lies a *nedotiopa'*" (*PSS*, 17: 94).

12. Konstantin Stanislavsky, in *Chekhov v vospominaniakh sovremennikov*, ed. N. I. Gitovich (Moscow: Khud. Lit., 1986), 407.

13. Harvey Pitcher, "Chekhov and the English Governess," *Oxford Slavonic Papers* 20 (1987): 101–9.

14. Chekhov, letter No. 3364.

15. Maria Chekhova, *Iz daliokogo proshlogo* (Moscow: Goslit., 1954), 215.

16. Note that *vishnia* means the sour, or Morello, cherry, which is usually cooked before it is eaten, as opposed to the sweet cherry (*chereshnia*). Really the play should be called *The Sour-Cherry Orchard*.

17. Tatiana Shchepkina-Kupernik, *Ezhegodnik Moskovskogo Khudozhestvennogo Teatra* (Moscow: Mkhat, 1944), 1: 531.

18. A very real fear, graphically expressed in 1898 (8–9 January) by Chekhov's elder brother Aleksandr, whose own play was taken off because of private intrigues in St. Petersburg: "The stage is managed and plays are switched by Kholeva, and Kholeva is managed by his concubine Domasheva. . . . In a word, our theater, headed by Iavorskaia [an ex-girlfriend of Anton Chekhov] is a pretty mangy cloaca, and God forbid one ever gets involved" (Aleksandr Pavlovich Chekhov, *Pis'ma A. P. Chekhov* (Moscow: Gos. Sots. Ekonom. lzd., 1939), 351.

19. M. Turovskaia, *Olga Leopardovna Knipper-Chekhova* (Moscow: Iskusstvo, 1972), 92.

20. Gorky offered 3,000 rubles (about $18,000 in today's currency) for the publishing rights.

21. V. I. Nemirovich-Danchenko, *Izbrannye pis'ma* (Moscow: Iskusstvo, 1954), 288.

22. K. S. Stanislavsky, *Sobranie sochinenii v 8-mi tomakh*, vol. 7 (Moscow: Iskusstvo, 1954), 277.

23. See Aleksandr Pavlovich Chekhov, *Pis'ma A. P. Chekhov*, 410–13. The racier letters have been censored, and the letters should be read in the RSL Archive, 331, 33, 24.

5. Act 1

1. Jovan Hristič, *Le Théâtre de Tchékhov* (Lausanne: L'Age d'Homme, 1982), 148–49, 171–73.

2. This is one of Chekhov's rare uses of a typical novelist's device to suggest an explosive dichotomy in a character by giving him or her a refined surname and a coarse Christian name, or vice versa: for instance, Flaubert's Emma Bovary.

3. To help us find our way in the text, however, we shall use the word *scene* to designate any section bounded by the entry or exit of a character: again, like a symphony, a Chekhov play is impossible to rehearse until it is broken down into sections with natural breaks. The French critic Louis Allain (in *Čechov: Werk und Wirkung*, ed. R. D. Kluge [Wiesbaden: Opera Slavica, 1990], 254–63) notes that characters' inquiries about, and references to, the time provide natural breaks in the acts, just like conventional scene divisions made by entries and exits.

4. The incident also develops the theme of perverse eating: a dog eat-

ing nuts, Ranevskaia eating crocodiles, and Pishchik consuming pills and, Firs alleges, half a bucket of cucumbers.

5. Compare Leskov's quoting Hippocrates: "What medicine won't cure, fire will cure. What fire won't cure, steel will cure. What steel won't cure, death will cure" (see A. S. Leskov, *Inzhenery-bessrebrenniki*, in *Sobranie sochinenii*, vol. 8 [Moscow: Khud. Lit.], 232–90). Chekhov had used the aphorism in a letter of 1886: "Russia has 174 poets. . . . From a medical point of view, this profusion is extremely ominous; if there are many treatments for a disease, then it is a very sure sign that the disease is incurable" (No. 208).

6. See *Rezhisserskie èkzempliary K. S. Stanislavskogo*, ed. I. N. Soloviova, vol. 3 (Moscow: Iskusstvo, 1983), 337.

7. Or so Stanislavsky says in his memoirs, *Chekhov v vospominaniakh sovremennikov*, 406–13.

6. Act 2

1. Villiers de l'Isle-Adam, *Axel* (Paris: Le Courrier du Livre, 1969), 249.

2. In Chekhov's original manuscript Ranevskaia's great speech is preceded by Charlotta, rifle on her back in the background, being dispatched by Varia to track down Ania and Trofimov. Understandably, Stanislavsky had this episode cut to preserve the dramatic tension.

3. Soloviova, ed., *Rezhisserskie èkzempliary K. S. Stanislavskogo*, 354.

4. Ibid., 349, 361.

5. The newspaper magnate Aleksei Suvorin, who was fond of Chekhov but deplored his liberalism, made a telling comment to the effect that Trofimov has learnt rhetoric from Gaev, even though Trofimov is a revolutionary and Gaev a liberal, thus recalling the father-son relationship in Dostoyevski's *The Devils* (1872), where the verbose liberal Stefan Verkhovensky has spawned, and is held responsible for, the subversive demagogy of his son Piotr (like Trofimov, "Petia" by nickname).

6. Soloviova, ed., *Rezhisserskie èkzempliary K. S. Stanislavskogo*, 359.

7. Ibid., 361.

8. The interpolation now begins with Ranevskaia ("A lot of use giants would be") and ends with Ania and Gaev saying, "There goes Epikhodov." In Chekhov's first revision, however, this episode went on with Varia saying, "Why is he living with us? He only walks and eats and drinks tea all day"; Lopakhin saying, "And he intends to shoot himself"; Ranevskaia saying, "But I like Epikhodov. When he talks about his misfortunes, he makes me laugh. Don't dismiss him, Varia"; and, finally, Varia responding, "We can't keep him, mama. We must dismiss him, he's good for nothing."

9. Soloviova, ed., *Rezhisserskie èkzempliary K. S. Stanislavskogo*, 363.

10. Compare the English "If a fitchew cross thy path and then an owl do cry / Make thy peace with God, poor soul, / For shortly thou shalt die."

11. Richard Peace in *The Four Major Plays* (New Haven, Conn.: Yale University Press, 1983) suggests that the Nadson poem is peculiarly appropriate because it ends with Ranevskaia's Christian name: "And love [*liubov'*] will return to earth" (180).

12. Soloviova, ed., *Rezhisserskie èkzempliary K. S. Stanislavskogo*, 365.

13. Lopakhin mispronounces Ophelia because he, like many Russians, cannot manage an *f* sound: his version, "Okhmelia," suggests the word *khmel'* (hops or drunkenness) and thus quietly brings in the motif of drunkenness, which is explicit at the end of act 3.

14. Stanislavsky, *Sobranie sochinenii v 8-mi tomakh*, 1: 270.

7. Act 3

1. Soloviova, ed., *Rezhisserskie èkzempliary K. S. Stanislavskogo*, 374–76.

2. In his notebooks (*Zapisnye knizhki* [Leningrad: Priboi, 1930], 184) Aleksandr Blok sketched an idea for a play very like *The Cherry Orchard*: "Central Russia. . . . In a landowner's house on the eve of destitution. At a family council everyone talks about loving their estate and being sorry to sell it. One holidays nowhere else. Another loves nature. A third—about love." Blok even had a ravine, a begging tramp, and "the vengeance of subterranean forces which have been roused."

3. Michel Saint-Denis, *Theatre: The Rediscovery of Style* (New York: Theater Arts Books, 1960), 42.

4. Quoted in Agate, *First Nights* (London, 1934), 215–16.

5. See Meierkhold, "Teatr. K istorii i tekhnike," in *Teatr. Kniga o novom teatre*, 143.

6. Stanislavsky, *Sobranie sochinenii v 8-mi tomakh*, 1: 267.

7. Here Stanislavsky had to give way to Chekhov: "Anton Pavlovich fears being too brusque and wants to tone it down. Therefore the candelabra nearly fell over. I think this is a half-measure. Let's have the candelabra fall and smash, but not on stage but out of sight in the hall" (in Soloviova, ed., *Rezhisserskie èkzempliary K. S. Stanislavskogo*, 427).

8. Act 4

1. Lopakhin consistently says *ty* to his inferiors—Epikhodov and the servants—and to Pishchik, presumably his drinking companion. But the Ranevskaia household, following contemporary French norms (and also the practice in Chekhov's house), avoids contemptuous familiarity toward servants. Only the old-fashioned Firs expects to be called *ty*. Iasha and Duniasha, despite the implicit seduction and abandonment, ape their masters and remain on formal *vy* terms throughout.

2. See Harai Golomb, "A Badenweiler View of Chekhov's Endings," in Kluge, 232–53, for this brilliant, original, and convincing argument.

9. The Metatext

1. Christian Morgenstern, *Palmström: Palma Kunkel* (Munich: DTV, 1961), 30.

2. Ibid., 31.

10. Intertexuality: Chekhov's Texts

1. *Vestnik Evropy* 7 (1988): 261.

2. *PSS*, 6: 260.

3. *PSS*, 8: 226–27.

4. *PSS*, 10: 203.

11. Intertexuality: Other Authors' Texts

1. See Leon Grossman *Turgenev* (Moscow: Goslitizdat, 1928).

2. Sacher-Masoch is mentioned in Chekhov's first play, *Platonov*. The Sacher-Masochian question of sexual dominance interested Chekhov as a doctor as well as a writer, even though the term *masochism* was not coined by Krafft-Ebing until after Chekhov's death.

3. By Robert Mann, in "The Breaking Clock: Chekhov and Goethe," *Germano-Slavica* 6, no. 2 (1988): 83–90.

12. The Aftermath

1. In his interview with Tom Driver, *Columbia University Forum* 4 (Summer 1961): 21–25.

Selected Bibliography

PRIMARY WORKS

Russian Texts

Polnoe sobranie sochinenii i pisem v 30i tomakh. Moscow: Nauka, 1974–83.
Chudakov, A. P. "Neprilichnye slova." *Literaturnoe obozrenie* 11 (1991):
  54–56. Includes censored letters and passages from Chekhov's writing.

English Translations

Hingley, R. *The Oxford Chekhov.* 9 vols. Oxford, New York, Toronto, and
  Melbourne: Oxford University Press, 1965–80. Includes major and
  minor stories.
Frayn, Michael. *Chekhov: Plays.* London and New York: Methuen, 1982;
  rev., 1988. Currently being revised for third edition.

SECONDARY WORKS

In English

Clyman, Toby W., ed. *A Chekhov Companion.* Westport, Conn., and London:
  Greenwood Press, 1985. A full bibliography up to 1984.
Gamble, Christine. "The English Chekhovians." Ph.D. diss. University of
  London, 1978.
Filips-Juswigg, Katherina. "Echoes of Chekhov's *The Cherry Orchard* in
  Foxfire." *Zapiski russkoi akademicheskoi gruppy v S.Sh.A.* 28 (1985):
  303–306.
Karlinsky, Simon. "Russian Anti-Chekhovians." *Russian Literature* 15 (1984):
  183–202.

Rayfield, D. "Chekhov and Popular Culture." *Irish Slavonic Studies* 9 (1988): 47–60.

———. "Chekhov's Orchard and Gardens." *Slavonic Review* 67, no. 3 (October 1989): 530–45.

Styan, J. L. *"The Cherry Orchard."* In *Critical Essays on Anton Chekhov*, edited by Thomas A. Eekman. Boston: G. K. Hall, 1989.

Terras, Victor. Bibliography. In *A Chekhov Companion*, edited by Toby W. Clyman, 180–83. Westport, Conn., and London: Greenwood Press.

Wellek, René, and N. Wellek. *Chekhov: New Perspectives.* Englewood Cliffs, N.J.: Prentice-Hall, 1984.

In Other Languages

Bonamour, J., V. B. Kataev, et al. *Tchékhoviana, Tchékhov et la France.* Paris and Moscow: Nauka, 1992.

Kluge, R. D., ed. *Čechov: Werk und Wirkung.* 2 vols. Wiesbaden: Opera Slavica, 1990.

Kuzicheva, A., et al. *Chekhoviana II & III.* Moscow: Nauka, forthcoming.

Lakshin, V., ed. *Chekhoviana.* Moscow: Nauka, 1990.

Reviakin, A. I. *"Vishniovyi sad" A. P. Chekhova.* Moscow: Iskusstvo, 1960.

Soloviova, I. N., ed. *Rezhisserskie èkzempliary K. S. Stanislavskogo.* Vol 3. Moscow: Iskusstvo, 1983.

Index

Index

The Author

Donald Rayfield was educated at Dulwich College and Cambridge University and is professor of Russian and Georgian at Queen Mary and Westfield College, University of London. He is the author of *Chekhov: The Evolution of His Art* (1975) and *The Dream of Lhasa: The Life of Nikolay Przhevalsky* (1976) and the translator of Vsevolod Garshin's stories and the anonymous *The Confessions of Victor X* (1982). He has also translated the verse of Osip Mandelstam and Vazha Pshavela, as well as Georgian folk poetry. He has completed a history of Georgian literature and is working on an integral study of Chekhov that will use recently released materials.

DATE DUE